LEARNING TO SOAR

Life Lessons for Those Facing Life's Challenges

J.E Bamidele Sturdivant

Learning to Soar

ISBN: 978-0-9831270-6-2

Published by

GodKulture Scrybes
A GodKulture Company
Chicago, Illinois

Phone: 815-630-9890

Email: gkscrybes@Godkulture.org

www.Godkulture.org | www.gkscrybes.com

Cover Design and Layout: **GodKulture**

Printed in United States of America

DEDICATION

This book is dedicated to every Parent, Pastor, Teacher, Care-Giver, Mentor and Coach who has selflessly believed in the potentiality of an individual despite the glaring deficiencies of their actuality! You'll never know how many lives you have both changed and saved. Your patient prodding was what someone needed to push them out of their insecurity and in to their destiny. Although they may never articulate it, they are eternally grateful. I know…I am one of them. THANK YOU!

The end of a thing is better than its beginning; the patient in spirit is better than the proud in spirit.

(Ecclesiastes 7:8)

SPECIAL THANKS

To my first born, J. Eric II, thank you for being my "second pair of eyes" during the writing, rewriting and editing process. You are gifted in so many areas that have proven to be a blessing to, not just the ministry, but me personally. I am extremely blessed to have you in my life, and honored to call you *son!*

ACKNOWLEDGMENTS

It is virtually impossible for me to express gratitude to those who have not just impacted my life, but are the reason that I am able to write this book. To all who have directly spoken to and encouraged me, or in your quiet time said a prayer for me, I thank you.

• **Segun Adebayo and Rotimi Kehinde:** You know how much I value my relationship with you. Blessings on the staff at GodKulture Scrybes and know that you are constantly in my prayers.

• **Bishop Alfred A. and Co-Pastor Susie C. Owens:** God bless you for the example you have set in marriage and the successful portrait of partners in ministry. How necessary that is in these times. God bless Mount Calvary.

• **My Siblings:** May this book bring a healing and peace to you that *surpasses all understanding.*

• **The Faith United Ministries family:** Thank you for the privilege of serving you. I look forward each week to releasing what God desires to give to you through me.

• **My children in the Lord:** God bless all of you for accepting me as your "spiritual" Dad. I will do my best not to fail you.

• **My mother, Lucille S.D. Sturdivant:** How do I express my appreciation to the one whose womb birthed me, hands guided me, voice taught me and example developed me? "THANK YOU" is not enough. I thank God *for* you and am proud that you are my mother.

• **Daddy G.O. and Mummy G.O.:** Words are inadequate when it comes to telling you what you mean to me. In time, I know the Almighty God will make clear the purpose of our connection. May the God of Elijah answer every one of your prayers by fire, and may He continue to perform miracles for RCCG, in Jesus' Mighty Name!

• **J.Eric, Joel, JaNeise and JaNette:** You are all grown now, but you'll always be my *babies*. I love you with and from a depth in me that I cannot describe. May you never have a day that you doubt the greatness that resides in you!

• **Finally, to my wife, Pam ("Modupe"):** What an honor it has been to be on this journey with you. Over thirty-eight years of being in my life, you've had to *live through* most of what I've been trying to *work through!* Only the Almighty God would know the perfect person necessary for Him to use in the process of perfecting me. I love you for your selflessness. I love you for your patience; I love you for believing in the *future* that I promised when I had just lost my job. Most of all…I love you for being you!

TABLE OF CONTENTS

FOREWORD

The plan of God for your life is to soar like an eagle. He wants you to easily, tirelessly and continuously fly above all the mountains of life, Isaiah 40: 31.

Why then are so many Christians bogged down? Why do many Christians spend most of their lives in the valley and even some in the pits and miry clays of life?

Pastor Sturdivant has the answers and the solutions. In this excellent book, he has done an in-depth study of why people crawl instead of fly like eagles. And he did not stop there. He shows you what you must do so that you may soar for the rest of your life. He even went further to show how those who are already flying could fly higher still.

This brilliant work is a must read for everyone. I am confident that by the time you finish reading this book, you will be surely and truly soaring.

I warmly recommend this book to you and all your friends.

Be blessed as you read.

E.A Adeboye

PREFACE

As the lion has been called "The King of the Beast", the eagle could justifiably be natures *royalty of the airways.* No other fowl so majestically and regally rules the sky. Solomon, the wisest man who ever lived, declares that there are a few things that he did not understand, and at the top of his chart was the eagle.

There are three things which are too wonderful for me, Yes, four which I do not understand: [19]*The way of an eagle in the air…*

(Proverbs 30:18-19)

When the Almighty God seeks to show His ability to deliver His children from whatever adversary or adversity that tries to keep them from attaining their destiny, He refers to the symbolism of an eagle.

You have seen what I did to the Egyptians, and how I bore you on eagles' wings and brought you to Myself.

(Exodus 19:4)

Further, the promise for every believer who has the ability to "… *wait on the Lord…*" is that they will ultimately "…mount up on wings like eagles…" (Isaiah 40:31)

Yet, this book, *Learning to Soar*, is not birthed from the glowing prospect of the eagle and its dominance. But rather, from a small phrase stated in the aforementioned text…*shall renew their strength…*

There is a period in the life of an eagle called the *molting stage*. It is at this point that he:

- Comes down to earth, due to the weight of (or lack of) his *old feathers*

- Pulls out his old feathers so that new ones can grow

- Beats his beak on a rock, which makes it difficult for him to 'express' himself or feed himself
- Loses his talons so that he cannot catch or *hold onto* anything
- Loses his *vision* during this period
- Associates with others in the same circumstance as himself

Many eagles die during this process. However, from time to time, one of these majestic birds who has *survived the process,* comes 'calling' over the place where the molting eagle has landed. This eagle, known as a *screaming eagle*, shouts encouragement to its struggling comrade and drops some food for him until he's able to fly again. This act by a *former* fellow molter, lets him know that:

- You are not forgotten
- You do have unexpected help
- The sky is awaiting your return
- This period is necessary for renewal

AH… the power of encouragement!

I am writing this book as a *screaming eagle*. One who has gone through the molting process, and *lived* to write about it. Maybe you have fallen or been dropped. Quite possibly you have gone through a period when you have had to suffer in silence or had your 'voice' hushed because of some abuse.

Maybe your vision and destiny has grown dim and no longer 'looks' attainable.

You could be the one who has lost so much until you no longer feel that you have a grip on life, thus you are simply going through the motions day by day.

I AM SCREAMING AT YOU!

You are *not* forgotten. There *is* help for you. The *process* was necessary for your *progress*. The sky, truly, is the limit. *I'll meet you in the air.*

J.E Bamidele Sturdivant

Section 1

RECOGNIZING LIFE'S CHALLENGES

Chapter One

A Crisis in Identity

MIDLIFE CRISIS

Although it is true that times change, one thing that has not changed over the years is that, at some point, many people across our nation, even the world, will suffer from an identity crisis. It is to the point where many even expect a midlife crisis as that fortieth or fiftieth birthday approaches and they begin to question the direction their lives have taken.

However, scripture reminds us that as people of God, there is only One, to whom we must look for our sense of purpose and identity. We must know who we are in Him.

But you are a chosen generation, a royal priesthood, a holy nation, His own special people, that you may proclaim the praises of Him who called you out of darkness into His marvelous light; [10]who once were not a people but are now the people of God, who had not obtained mercy but now have obtained mercy.

(1 Peter 2:9-10)

THWARTED PLANS

It is common for people to have goals which they hope to accomplish in life, but then face an issue which disrupts their plans. This disruption often precipitates a crisis in identity.

When my high school graduation approached, over thirty years ago now, I knew I wanted to be an attorney, although I am not sure why.

Perhaps it was because I wanted to talk a lot, or maybe I simply wanted to defend the innocent. I just knew that I wanted to be a lawyer. At that time, there were not any well-known attorneys such as the late Johnny Cochran. Probably the most famous example of a lawyer we knew of was Perry Mason, a fictious character on television, played by the late Raymond Burr.

Regardless, I knew that I wanted to be a lawyer, and my mother promised she would save money for me to go to college. My grandmother also said that she would set aside money to help me achieve my heart's desire. However, over time, the situation in my family changed. My mother had to use the money she had saved for the fifth child, me, on the previous four. So the money for college I had been counting on was not available.

In addition, unbeknownst to us, my grandmother had begun to slip into Alzheimer's disease (although that name for the disease was not known at that time). Sadly, some of the various people she had invited into her home had taken advantage of her, stealing her money and possessions. As a result, the money she had set aside for my education was not there either.

So though I knew I wanted to be a lawyer, suddenly there I was at age eighteen just out of high school, but life and family issues shattered my dream and caused that goal to appear impossible. Those things that I thought would be available to help me become *who* I thought I was supposed to be were gone.

All of a sudden, I was having an identity crisis.

NOW WHAT?

Unfortunately, at that time no one told me if there was actually money available for young people in my situation.

Remember, that was more than thirty-five years ago. I did not know whether or if grants were available at that time. All I knew was that what I could accomplish was based on what my mother had the ability to provide, which was no longer available.

So this lack of knowledge caused me to begin to wander through life, unable to accomplish anything. For a while, I was doing some stage work – singing and performing in plays, which was good, but not good enough, because that was not *the plan.*

But at twenty years old, I was no longer able to perform in those high school plays, because I was no longer in high school. What was I to do?

IT'S A SET UP

There is no instruction manual that tells us what to do after we turn eighteen. Although we are expected to act as adults, we have been living in our parents' house, under our parents' rules, for eighteen years. The transition is not easy, and is doubly difficult if you come from a home with the various dysfunctions that existed in the 'average' family then and now.

Yet, somehow society makes us think that a burst of common sense occurs simply because a particular birthday has been reached.

When my children were in college, I had to meet with the administrators on campus at a particular university in order to sign the paperwork agreeing to pay for their tuitions. However, when I tried to go to those administrators to discuss certain struggles my children were undergoing, they said "Sorry, your children have to take care of these themselves, because they're adults."

Yet, these were the same children who had no responsibility, who just yesterday were doing nothing more than picking their clothes up off the floor, the same ones whose sole responsibility were basic chores: to operate a washing machine, work a part-time job and make up a bed!

Though their bodies had announced with pubic hair and breasts that they were mature, they still did not have "grown up" mature common sense. How could they? They were just finishing high school!

It is amazing how society sets up young people to make adult decisions with immature teenage minds. Then these same young people spend the majority of their lives trying to get out of the situations resulting from their childish reasoning's – decisions they never would have made if they had had enough sense not to try to be grown before they were ready.

WHO AM I?

After graduation, I went through a phase of saying that I had to "find myself"; not because I had "lost" myself, but because everything I had hung my hopes on had changed. I have discovered that the root problem of our identity crisis, however, is not in *finding* ourselves but in *knowing* ourselves. We must know who we are in order to lose who we are. To "find" ourselves implies that we once knew ourselves, but then lost ourselves somewhere.

This loss of identity has truly become a crisis in today's society. Men are trying to be women, getting breast implants and dressing like females. Then there are women trying to be men, wearing their pants hanging off their behinds or trying to "take care' of another female, calling her "wife".

The fact that these individuals seem compelled to exaggerate their newly acquired femininity or masculinity makes it obvious that these actions are not natural.

Moreover sons and daughters of upscale Caucasians are listening to rap and urban music and trying to mimic what they have heard from inner city youths. In other cultures, young people wear the brand of hip-hop artists and try to imitate their rap music. Young women dress more and more provocatively, while old women try to dress like young women.

Old men are trying to hang out with young girls – there is nothing more foolish than an old guy trying to act like he is a young stud. Most recently, grown men and women everywhere want to throw off their responsibilities and act like adolescents again.

But we cannot keep doing the things we did twenty years ago! If we wore hip huggers twenty years ago, this is not our turn; even if they call them "low riders" now. That is not who we are anymore.

All over the world, people are going about *finding* their identities in all the wrong ways. And most of us live in the midst of this confusion every day *without knowing* how very foolish it is.

I'M BEGGING YOU…

The worst part of this identity crisis is that it is not merely a problem that exists in the world, but also in the Body of Christ, despite the fact that the source of our identity should be completely different from the world's.

I beseech you therefore, brethren, by the mercies of God, that you present your bodies a living sacrifice, holy, acceptable to God, which is your reasonable service. [2]And do not be conformed to this world, but be transformed by the renewing of your mind, that you may prove what is that good and acceptable and perfect will of God. [3]For I say, through the grace given to me, to everyone who is among you, not to think of himself more highly than he ought to think, but to think soberly, as God has dealt to each one a measure of faith.

(Romans 12:1-3)

The Living Bible translates the first two verses of the same passage this way:

And so, dear brothers, I plead with you to give your bodies to God. Let them be a living sacrifice, wholly, the kind He can accept when you think of what He has done for you. Is this too much to ask? Don't copy the behavior and customs of this world but be a new and different person with a fresh newness in all you do and think. Then you will learn from your own experience how His ways will really satisfy you.

Notice Paul's use of the words *brethren* and *brothers*. He is not addressing sinners in this passage; he is exhorting the saints in the Body of Christ not to "copy the behavior and customs of this world"

WHAT IS NORMAL ANYHOW?

So often the reason it is difficult to get people from the world to come to church is because the same issues troubling the world are occurring in the church. For example the divorce rate is higher in the church now than it is in the world.

We so often hear the excuse "the church is full of hypocrites" – and to some extent, it is true. It seems everyone who has acted as a "Slick Willy", "Pimp Daddy" or "Freaky Freda" in the world is trying to be the same Slick Willy, Pimp Daddy and Freaky Freda in the church.

Despite their membership in the Body of Christ, they are still holding the world as the source of their identities. It seems like almost everyone is immoral and impure, without scruples or standards.

This immorality cannot be explained away as merely struggling when so many are not even trying to live righteously. Instead, they claim they are simply trying to be normal, like everyone else.

However, if by being "normal" they hope to be like the world, then those individuals are actually on a downward spiral to eternal destruction, for the Word tells us that *that* is the final resting place for those caught up in the world.

The command, "*do not be conformed to this world*" indicates we are to be in the world but we cannot let it get in us. A boat sinks when the water that the boat is floating on gets into the boat. Just because we are in the world does not mean we act like the world.

We cannot allow what others do to cause us to think we ought to do the same. God created us as individuals.

A HIGHER STANDARD

As members of the Body of Christ we are a chosen generation, a royal priesthood, and Gods special people (I Peter 2:9)! God is calling us to something higher than the world's "normal". To the world our normal is their supernatural. It is not normal for us to struggle as we do! It is not normal for us to be sick, broke, lonely or to continuously live in despair.

It may be worldly, but it is not normal for a believer, because a child of God does not operate within the same standards as the world. This higher standard means that when we ask for favor of God, we must understand that He answers us on condition.

In other words, He blesses based on whether we meet His requirements. If we do not meet His requirements, He cannot do what we have asked, no matter how many times we fast, no matter how many times we fall on our faces to cry. God is not moved by our emotions, He (as He commands us) must honor the standard of His word.

If we are not doing what He has required, He is not obligated to fulfill His word.

LEARN TO SOAR

The world's pull on us is indeed powerful. Is it possible to avoid its siren song? Are we truly able to live up to God's higher standard? The answers to these and many more important questions are contained in the remaining chapters of this text.

Friend, it is my hope that this book will provide you with the tools necessary to break free from the world's influence and from the wiles of the devil. My prayer is that you are free to receive all the blessings God has in store for you – so that you may *LEARN TO SOAR*!

PRAYER POINT

Father! Help me to gain my identity from how You made me, and not from events or environments that try to define me! In Jesus' Mighty Name, Amen!

SCRIPTURE REFERENCE:

Psalm 139: 14-16

Chapter Two

Breaking the World's Mold

NOW YOU SEE IT, NOW YOU DON'T

If God is the source of your identity, you do not truly know who you are if you are basing your identity on the circumstances you see surrounding you. In other words, you cannot merely "call it like you see it" in regards to the situations in your life. You have to call it like you *want it to be!* God gave Adam the power to call the things around him whatever he desired them to be.

Out of the ground the LORD God formed every beast of the field and every bird of the air, and brought them to Adam to see what he would call them. And whatever Adam called each living creature that was its name.

(Genesis 2:19)

Likewise you have the power to call your situations what they should be before they become what you have called them. You cannot wait until you see it and then say "it is what it is". You must declare what it is and then you will see it. You are healed even if you are in pain, even if the doctor says there is no cure. You are rich even if you do not have two nickels to rub together.

YOU ARE WHAT YOU THINK

Proverbs 23:7 teaches, *"for as he thinks in his heart so is he"*. This means that *the problems that you face are not actually the problem*. The real problem is your mind, how you think. For example, you could move into a wonderful roomy house, but if you still have a one bedroom apartment mindset, you will live in one room and the rest of that wonderful house will fall into disrepair.

One can usually tell what a person thinks about himself by looking at those with whom he associates. If you are afraid to introduce your friends to anyone, not only are you ashamed of who *they* are, but you are also ashamed of letting anyone else know who *you* really are. In other words, you are living a life of deception. Check your environment. Look at the people with whom you associate and the places you enjoy. You will quickly discover *your true identity..*

PUT THE PAST BEHIND YOU

Let us look back at the command, *do not be conformed.* Notice the word "conform" contains the word "con". When we are not truthful, we are said to be trying to *con, dupe, or swindle* those around us; we present something that is not real. We cannot allow the world to change who we know ourselves to be.

It is possible for an individual to seemingly know who they are and what they want out of life; then have a tragedy, a misstep, or simply make a *bad* choice, and find it difficult to regain their footing and their focus.

The truth is, that in order to find one's self, you may have to revisit a place in your emotions, your past, quite possibly a place of pain - in order to begin recovering.

Sure, you can stop thinking about it and put it behind you, but unless you know what made you get to that place, the same spirit will cause you to go to places just like that over and over again. If you never deal with *why* you do what you do, you will persist in that pattern continuously…simply in another arena.

LIKE PLAY-DOUGH IN THE POTTER'S HANDS

O house of Israel, can I not do with you as this potter?" says the LORD. "Look, as the clay is in the potter's hand, so are you in My hand, O house of Israel!

(Jeremiah 18:6)

Since we are like putty in God's hands, the implication is that it is easy for us to take on the shape of whatever mold in which we end up, even if it is not Gods mold. When I was younger, we used to have Play-dough. I would put my Play-dough inside of a machine and crank the little handle, and the Play-dough would come out in the shape of a star, a circle, a ball, or whatever shape was set as the pattern.

The Play-dough would become that shape because of the pressure that I put on it when I turned the crank. Likewise, you can, if you are not prayerful and careful, become the shape of those around you because of pressure that is put on you – peer pressure, boyfriend or girlfriend pressure, or "have a drink" pressure or free sex pressure.

Whatever the pressure may be, if there is enough of it, you will conform to it if you do not know who you are and who you are supposed to be. You will take on the shape of whatever you are pressed against.

BREAKING THE MOLD

Here is the good news, it is possible to avoid the world's mold. The following passages give us three steps.

For I say, through the grace given to me, to everyone who is among you, not to think of himself more highly than he ought to think, but to think soberly, as God has dealt to each one a measure of faith.

(Romans 12:3)

First we are told "not to think of ourselves more highly than we ought to think".

The Living Bible says; *be honest of your estimate of yourself.* In other words, **YOU MUST HAVE AN HONEST ASSESSMENT OF BOTH YOUR STRENGTHS AND WEAKNESSES**. The only thing that keeps you from having these honest assessments is pride. This is when you arrogantly think you are so much stronger than you are and that you can handle situations you really cannot handle.

Here is pride, you believe that you have the ability to walk into certain places or keep certain company and walk right out again unharmed and unaffected. And once you have frequented those places once or twice, you figure they will never affect you. You wrongly believe that you can be in the company of certain people and their ways will not "rub off" on you.

In truth, whoever you associate with, you will eventually emulate. If you befriend those who have no goals for the future, then your friends will always be people without vision for their lives. And if they are "tougher" in their weakness than you are in your strength, they will pull you to where they are before you "lift" them to where you are.

That is why the scripture teaches us to come out from among them, to not even associate with those individuals.

THE DEVIL'S ADVOCATE

A few years ago Keanu Reaves starred in a movie called *The Devil's Advocate*. Keanu plays a small-time lawyer in a small town who has dreams of "making it big". But his dreams do not include going through the process to get to where he wants to be. So instead he begins making underhanded deals.

He even defends people that he knows are guilty, and covers up their guilt. He overrides opportunities to love his wife, to be faithful and loyal to her. He ultimately accomplishes his "dream" of success, fame and security. But it cost him his wife. Eventually she loses her mind and kills herself.

Finally, Keanu tries to say that the devil made him do all those deceitful things.

Al Pacino, who plays the devil in the person of his lawyer/mentor/boss, replies "No, no, no, I told you over and over again that you needed to be more loving and faithful to your wife. I told you to take a break, that it was okay to lose, but you said, 'I don't lose'. Don't blame it on me; I told you".

At the end of the movie, Keanu gets a chance to start all over again. He is taken back to his humble small town beginnings. He revisits the place where he "lost himself". The devil comes in, disguised as a different person, a reporter, to give him another opportunity, and this times Keanu says, "No, I'm not going to do it".

But as he gets pushed a little bit more, he finally says, "I'll think about it. Call me in the morning". The devil's final line is so telling: "Vanity, my favorite tool"

SAME DEVIL, DIFFERENT DISGUISE

When God gives us another chance, we must realize that the devil will soon be back in a different disguise, also giving us another chance, appealing to that area of vanity (pride) of our lives. Overconfidence in yourself makes you underestimate your enemy.

When you overestimate yourself, you are susceptible to the "that will never happen to me", trap.

"I'll never get involved with a married person. I'll never commit adultery'.

"I'll never get high."

"I'll never lie like that"

Unfortunately, however, the very things that one arrogantly says he or she will never do are the very things that they will eventually stumble into. Why? The enemy *takes* pride in using *your* pride against you.

YOU'LL FALL FOR ANYTHING

Therefore let him who thinks he stands take heed lest he fall.

(1 Corinthians 10:12)

If we do not take heed, we are setting ourselves up for a fall. Why? Because,

Pride goes before destruction, And a haughty spirit before a fall.

(Proverbs 16:18)

The moment you believe nothing can bring you down is the moment you are about to fall into something.

For if anyone thinks himself to be something, when he is nothing, he deceives himself.

(Galatians 6:3)

If your flesh brags that you are more than you are, where can you find the honest assessment of your strengths and weaknesses you need in order to avoid the world's mold? Proverbs 3: 5-7 contains the solution:

Trust in the LORD with all your heart, And lean not on your own understanding; [6]*In all your ways acknowledge Him, And He shall direct your paths.* [7]*Do not be wise in your own eyes; Fear the LORD and depart from evil.*

Only the Lord in His wisdom knows our true strengths.

SOBRIETY CHECKPOINT

Secondly, if we are not going to allow the world to mold us, we must "*think soberly*". When you hear that word *sober*, you usually think of its contrast, drunk. But what "to think soberly" means is that ***you must not allow momentary experiences to intoxicate you***.

There are so many who are jumping and shouting and praising, but not living holy lives, still struggling with their identities, still unable to clean up their credit, not making any impact in the kingdom. Your identity in Christ is not all about the jumping and shouting and praising, it is about how steadily you run the race.

You must get into a place where you walk worthy of what God has given you to do. *The mismanagement of moments is what leads to a lifetime of regrets.* Remember that statement; it is powerful!

When you allow a momentary thing to intoxicate you without considering its repercussions, you have the potential of ruining your life through that one moment.

The enemy will let you have victory in that one moment so that he can weaken you to drop your guard for the next moment. Those of you whose lives are off track today got that way through mismanaged moments. It was what you did minute by minute by minute.

The reason you are so needy, so codependent, so immature is because when you had a moment to do something right, you allowed your imagined strength to intoxicate you and make you believe you had the ability to handle certain things, when in reality you did not.

TOLERANCE IS NOT THE ANSWER

The opposite of being sober is to be intoxicated. For some people, intoxication manifests itself by the way they stagger, when they walk. Others urinate on themselves. Some fall down; some throw up. Others get loud or belligerent. Some instantly become the "life of the party" while others get depressed. Some people say, "I can drink a little bit more because I have high tolerance for alcohol". Well, the enemy has higher levels of sin to pull them down too.

Instead of being so busy trying to prove it won't *affect* you, you should be saying, "Why don't I stay away from it before it *infects* me? There are some things I know I cannot try. There are some places I know I cannot go. There are some people with whom I know I cannot associate". There must be an honest assessment so that we do not ruin a destiny because of a momentary lapse.

INTOXICATION ANTIDOTE

So what is the antidote for intoxication?

See then that you walk circumspectly, not as fools but as wise, [16]redeeming the time, because the days are evil. [17]Therefore do not be unwise, but understand what the will of the Lord is. [18]And do not be drunk with wine, in which is dissipation; but be filled with the Spirit.

(Ephesians 5:15-18)

The opposite of being intoxicated by a moment is to be filled with the Spirit. Rather than allowing something from outside (the world) to get inside of you, instead be filled from the inside with the Spirit, who transforms the way you walk outside.

When you get ready to go somewhere you should not be, the Holy Ghost will set off an alarm in you, "No, no, no, you cannot go there". The problem is that many really don't want to live like God wants us to live. There was a bumper sticker out some years ago that used to say, "How much wrong can I do and still make it to heaven?".

Most of us are living our lives trying to figure out exactly what sin we can commit, what are the consequences, and what we can get away with. Instead of saying, "it's a sin. I'm not going to do it", we wonder "*Why* it is a sin?" That single moment of questioning God's standard serves as a *doorway* of entry for the enemy's deception.

If you are questioning God, your problem is deeper than wanting to know His will. You are trying to force Him to change His will to accommodate your "won't's". You *won't* live holy, you *won't* pray, and you *won't do His will.*

Instead change your won'ts to his will!

HALF A CUP OF FAITH

As God has dealt to each one a measure of faith.

(Romans 12:3b)

Finally, to avoid conforming to the world's mold, ***we must operate in the level of faith that we have been given.*** Not everyone has the same measure of faith. Jesus told a story about how one man had one talent, one had two, and one had five. Everyone had something but they did not have all the same amount.

They received based on what their employer knew they had an *ability* or capability, rather, to handle. But each had at least one. Neither the size nor amount of your faith is the key; it is utilizing whatever size or amount you have. According to 2 Corinthians 5:7; *we walk by faith, not by sight.* It is only as you walk with God or develop relationship with Him that your faith grows.

I can say "by tomorrow *this* is going to happen" and for me it is true, because my faith can believe it. But if you have not walked with God and been through what I have been through to gain that same measure of faith, you may say it, but it will not be true for you. Listen, your faith grows as you develop your relationship with the One who has given you the *measure of faith.*

YOUR FAITH NEEDS A WORKOUT

Scripture also tells us; *Faith without works is dead* (James 2:20), if you are not working with the faith you have, then it is dead. As your ability to deal with various issues is based on faith you have established in your walk with God, you need faith that is alive! Different levels of faith mean, there are some things that other people can try and accomplish for the kingdom that you may be too spiritually *immature* to attempt.

Although you may be the same age as that person, the same size, etc., if you do not have the faith walk with God that they have, you cannot handle the same things. I raised my children in church and in a Christian school, and then I put them in a public high school so that they could be prepared for life outside of a sheltered environment.

Their foundation was not *world*, it was *Word*, but when they got into the secular school system, they were suddenly dealing with people whose foundation was *world*, not *Word.*

The pressure from a secular arena was greater than the "level" of their faith walk. And so in an effort to get along with the world, they tried to compromise the Word. I had them in a situation their faith was not yet big enough to handle.

YOU CAN'T HANDLE IT

There is a difference between somebody who can *do* "street" and somebody who was *born* "street'. Those born street (meaning streetwise or savvy) will manipulate and use those of us who were not. They will take advantage of us every time.

Yet, many insist in associating with people that are not in their league. Then they spend the rest of their lives trying to recover. When this happens, you have a tendency to act like something you never were, trying to fit in, in hopes that you will be accepted, because the world has made you think that your testimony has got to be, "God *delivered me from*". So you claim to be a child of God while still trying to act like the world. You figure since God can use *everyone*, it does not matter how many piercings, tattoos, babies, etc. you have.

Yes, God *is* going to draw people in *from* the world with all those issues. But He is certainly not expecting those already in church to act like the world and then hang on to the worlds coattails in order to get back to Him. Truly, the greatest testimony is, "God *kept me* from doing this and that." Why? Because every place you have been is just one less place you will not have to search when you have lost yourself.

IT'S MY OWN FAULT

I was at the car wash recently. As I was about to get into my car, a man walked up to me and said, "Brother Sturdivant, I recognize you from a long time ago. I'm one of the original members of a particular church; I used to play the drums, but by my own choosing, I walked away from God. It wasn't anybody's fault. I did it"

Keep in mind, I did not know this man; he knew me. But the Holy Spirit had led him to begin confessing. I said, "Son you are closer to being where you're supposed to be than ever before because you aren't blaming it on anyone else but yourself.'

He said, "I'm at a point right now where I don't even enjoy getting high but I can't stop. I'm all right in the daytime. Like right now, while I'm by myself, I'm okay. But as soon as I go home and get in my environment, I know I'm going to start doing the same thing again. I get into trouble because I'm always in the wrong places. You see this long cut down the side of my face?"

"Yeah."

He said, 'Some guys who didn't know me from a can of paint just walked behind me and hit me, broke my jaw.

I had to have surgery and everything, just because I was somewhere I didn't have any business being, doing what I didn't even enjoy."

LEARNING THE LESSON

What can we learn from this man's story? First, we see that his experiences forced him to become honest with himself regarding his weaknesses, and he came to realize that there were places and situations he could not handle.

We must go further, however. An honest estimate of ourselves allows us to go beyond merely avoiding situations and places, to soberly walking out our faith moment by moment.

PRAYER POINT

Father! Keep me on Your designing wheel, pressing and shaping me, until I am the vessel that You've purposed me to be. In Jesus' Mighty Name, Amen!

SCRIPTURE REFERENCE:

Romans 9:21

Chapter Three

Uncovering Your Family Resemblance

I find daytime television to be an interesting phenomenon. On the rare occasion when my curiosity is piqued and I chose to view one of the typical daytime shows, I am constantly amazed at the stupidity and immorality of the participants who are willing to air their private business on television.

Sadly, the daytime talk show industry makes its profits by displaying these people's misfortunes. Most of the shows (after a while all of them have the same format) make their names and ratings through the torrid display of infidelities, betrayals, broken promises and unfaithfulness of those who, for a "free trip" to the city of the program and a hotel stay, will discuss behaviors and display attitudes that you would not believe even existed.

WHO'S YOUR DADDY?

I am particularly amazed by the participants on the "talk" shows that have young couples on them. Their highest ratings occur when they feature a woman with low self-esteem and no morals who has slept with so many men that she has no idea who her baby's father is.

So she brings out a line of men – brainless, hairless, even toothless in some cases – who may or may not have fathered her child but obviously, have had sex with her.

Then her baby's picture is compared to the men in question, and the woman eventually claims she knows the father, because they have the same nose, or mouth or some other feature. But what's interesting is, once the DNA is tested, the results are usually quite different. And often the woman will testify, "Well, I really *wanted* him to be the one".

Other times, the host features a couple and their child, and the woman will say to the man who has been raising this child from birth, "I've got something to tell you. Even though you thought differently, this child may not be yours"

What a messy situation!

IT DOESN'T MATTER WHAT YOU WISH FOR

As I began studying the following scripture passage, I realized that this text is actually a biblical version of those daytime talk shows!

Here is someone claiming a particular person as their father, but there is no family resemblance. There is no way this person can actually be their father, because they have all the traits and attributes, the DNA, of someone else; no matter how much they wish he was their father.

They answered and said to Him, "Abraham is our father." Jesus said to them, "If you were Abraham's children, you would do the works of Abraham. 40*But now you seek to kill Me, a Man who has told you the truth which I heard from God. Abraham did not do this.* 41*You do the deeds of your father." Then they said to Him, "We were not born of fornication; we have one Father—God."* 42*Jesus said to them, "If God* *were your Father, you would love Me, for I proceeded forth and came from God; nor have I come of Myself, but He sent Me.* [43]*Why do you not understand My speech? Because you are not able to listen to My word.* [44]*You are of your father the devil, and the desires of your father you want to do. He was a murderer from the beginning, and does not stand in the truth, because there is no truth in him. When he speaks a lie, he speaks from his own resources, for he is a liar and the father of it.* [45]*But because I tell the truth, you do not believe Me.* [46]*Which of you convicts Me of sin? And if I tell the truth, why do you not believe Me?* [47]*He who is of God hears God's words; therefore you do not hear, because you are not of God."*

(John 8:39-47)

In this text, Jesus is attempting to explain to the religious leaders that their argument does not necessarily determine who their father is. He clearly lays out the criteria for overcoming the confusion of their spiritual lineage.

The leaders claim that they are from Abraham, but Jesus explains that that may be where they claim that they came from, but what they do and how they conduct themselves towards Him really determines who their father is.

In other words, in the beginning they were loyal to Abraham. But as time passed, they descended from that place; they fell from Abraham's standards for his family.

They are not his children.

WHAT HAVE YOU DONE LATELY?

Those of us who are parents know that there are some things that children do that do not resemble any part of their upbringing. Although my father was not around to raise me, the effects of his life choices had an impact on my life choices. As an adult, I discovered that when I was a child, I had certain traits of my father that I did not even know about.

My father had opened a spiritual door for certain things to be in the family line; even if we never saw them, or him, our bloodline was tainted by them. So I came into the picture fighting issues I was not even aware of. Someone once said, "Blood is thicker than water". However *spirit* is thicker than blood.

Similarly, for someone reading this book, even now you may be dealing with issues that were never a part of your upbringing, but are in your bloodline nonetheless, because your parents opened that door somewhere along the line.

And if you cannot deal with what your parents have done and you just hate *them* for it, you will wind up becoming the very thing you hate. This struggle is more than emotional, it is spiritual. As such, there is a way of ridding oneself of a spiritual legacy of negativity that has been left in the bloodline. Victory is possible!

IS IT IN YOU?

The first criterion of your spiritual parentage is: **HOW MUCH WORD DO YOU HAVE IN YOU?**

I know that you are Abraham's descendants, but you seek to kill Me, because My word has no place in you.

(John 8:37)

Sadly many of us do not even crack our Bibles until Sunday. Surprisingly, many preachers do not open their Bibles until they have to preach. God's Word is His will, and His identity is found in his Word. *You cannot know how to look like God if you never read his Word.*

THE UNIVERSITY OF GOD

The book of Genesis says that Adam named every animal that was brought to him. Have you ever wondered where he learned the names? Obviously he never attended any university. Adam knew what to do because he was made in the image of *all knowledge*, Omniscience. Since he was made in God's image, he simply said what God knows.

Before sin, before the Fall, man knew everything God knows. There was no such thing as "I don't know how to get my life together". Now, post-Fall, we no longer know what God knows. So we use education for information, when what we really need is revelation. *Education is a descendant of revelation.*

Whatever you do not know, the Holy Ghost discerns and tells you. So there are certain things you will know without understanding *how* you know, because the Spirit of Truth dwells in you. The more you sin, however, the less you are open to hear because your spiritual ears become spiritually clogged with the wax of the world. So the more you sin, the less you know. And the more you sin the more you lose your identity. So you end up trying to use education to get your identification.

WHO ARE YOU? I DON'T RECOGNIZE YOUR VOICE

When I was younger, I used to preach forty revivals a year, starting on Sunday with family day and going all the way through Friday; forty weeks out of a year. Mind you, there are only fifty-two weeks in a year! I will never forget one day when I came home and said, "I'm home" and all of my children said "Mommy?" because they did not recognize my voice. I had been travelling so much they had gotten used to the voice of their mother and had forgotten the voice of their father.

Similarly, it is possible for us to be away so long, that when God tries to call, we do not recognize His voice. Who has had your time and attention so long that their voice is more recognizable than God's? What *voices* bombard your psyche so much that the Master cannot reach you? Shut out the world and say as Samuel, "Speak, Lord, Your servant is listening" (1 Samuel 3:10).

TALK THE TALK, WALK THE WALK

I speak what I have seen with My Father, and you do what you have seen with your father.

(John 8:38)

The second criterion of one's true parentage is: **WHAT DO MY ACTIONS SAY?** In other words, you can tell who your real father is by how you talk and what you do. What is the first thing that comes out of your mouth when something goes wrong? What is the first thing you do? How do you respond under pressure?

Miriam Webster's Dictionary explains that "resemblance" means a similarity in nature, form or appearance. *Nature* speaks to what my natural proclivity or inclination is. In other words, if someone gets on my nerves, if I am under pressure, what reaction comes *naturally*? Natural inclination has to do with what you do without thinking; it is what you do habitually, without thinking that indicates your true parentage.

THE PLACE WE GO, THE PEOPLE WE SEE

Form makes reference to what shapes or molds you. What is your environment? Where you assemble and who you associate with, are evidence of who your father is. We discussed in the previous chapter that naturally we want to think that we can walk into any situation and walk out all right.

But just as when the television is on, even if you are "not watching" eventually you are going to be taking it in. That is why it is called "tel"-e-"vision." It will "*tell a vision*." It will tell you what to look for in stores; it will tell you how you should view yourself and how you should think.

Where there is no vision, the people perish (Proverbs 29:18), but where there is a vision from the world, the repercussions are worse.

Environment does not just mean the things that are around you, it also means the situations and places you put yourself into. There are some places you frequent that make God's voice come out like white noise. It is staticky or indiscernible.

THE WRONG FREQUENCY

After my vehicle has been in the shop I can tell that the mechanics have been in it. When I turn on my radio, it is on another station; someone had changed my frequency. So for that brief moment, I am forced to listen to whatever is on until I change the station.

And if I am not careful, my old nature starts to remember and love what I am listening to. You must always remember that the old nature wants sin more that righteousness. Understand, the mechanics who have been in my care are not bad men.

Their desires and taste in music are just no good for *me*. Likewise, there are some people in your life that might not really be bad, but they are not good for you.

The environment you allow yourself to participate in speaks volumes.

LOOK AT ME!

Resemblance also speaks to *appearance.* How closely do we resemble our Father in appearance?

Sadly, we often dress better to go to dinners, clubs and sporting events than we do to come to church. Why do we give God such low grade and then give the devil our best? We ought to give God our best. Recently, I caught a heavyweight fight on television. I was amazed at the fashion show that went on there!

People had rented Bentley's and Rolls Royce's. Even the pregnant girls who were there had special dresses made. Just for an event that was not even worth the price of the ticket! My best might not be your best, but even if you are dressed in your only pair of jeans, make sure that they look presentable when you come into the Lord's house.

DON'T RUN AWAY

But now you seek to kill Me, a Man who has told you the truth which I heard from God. Abraham did not do this.

(John 8:40)

The third criterion to trace one's spiritual parentage is: **CAN YOU FACE THE TRUTH?** A person who is God's child does not run from hearing the truth. It is evident whether or not you are actually God's child by how you deal with the truth. If you cannot handle the truth, it means that you prefer a lie. And who is a liar and the father of lies? …you do the math.

Often many are running from what they *know* to be true; they simply thought that nobody else knew it. So when someone calls them out, publicizing what they thought was a hidden part of them, they want to run.

Then, the natural reaction is to try to assassinate the "messenger", their name, or their character.

Perhaps every time a sermon hits home with you, you become agitated and feel a sudden need to take a sabbatical from church. You must understand the timing of your irritation. The devil never gets irritated or upset until someone confronts him with who he is, what he is doing and why he is doing it. Once he is called out, he will immediately try to make *you* place the blame on everyone else rather than take responsibility for what *he* has done.

DO YOU HEAR WHAT I AM SAYING?

Why do you not understand My speech? Because you are not able to listen to My word.

(John 8:43)

Herein lies the fourth criterion. It is not that you are not intelligent enough to know Jesus is telling you the truth; it is just that **YOU HAVE SELF-INFLICTED IGNORANCE**. You have decided, not that you *cannot* hear what He is saying, but that you *will not* receive it. Therefore, every time the truth comes out, you claim, "I just don't receive it. I rebuke that"

But whether you receive it or not does not change the fact that it is truth. There are those who choose to be ignorant because, to know the truth would force them to change. Therefore they do no read the Word, listen to gospel music or attend Bible study. Why? Because they think that by avoiding these things will excuse them from responsibility and punishment when they stand before God.

But Scripture is clear to the contrary:

And that servant who knew his master's will, and did not prepare himself or do according to his will, shall be beaten with many stripes.

(Luke 12:47)

For since the creation of the world His invisible attributes are clearly seen, being understood by the things that are made, even His eternal power and Godhead, so that they are without excuse.

(Romans 1:20)

ARE YOU HUNGRY?

This portion reveals the fifth criterion, which is: **YOUR DESIRES WILL REVEAL YOUR DADDY**.

You are of your father the devil, and the desires of your father you want to do.

(John 8:44a)

What do you hunger for? I am not talking about steak and potatoes, but what is it that you are always gravitating towards? What is it that makes you comfortable? How do you spell "relief"? The Bible says, "*...those who hunger and thirst after righteousness shall be filled" (Matthew 5:6)* Do you have an appetite that has nothing to do with God? Instead of the living Word, do you crave luxury and wealth; do you want crystal meth instead of Christ?

Maybe you are hungering after your career, chasing after the trappings of success, trying to fill the emptiness inside. You have a hunger for the wrong thing. You cannot be satisfied. There will always be a "place" in you that only the presence of the Almighty can fill.

If you start hungering after God, however, signs and wonders will follow you.

When Adam was created in the image and likeness of God, he did not have to look for a job. A job was placed under him. He did not have to try to find a mate. He woke up one morning and his mate was standing right there. This is the design God had for us.

But seek first the kingdom of God and His righteousness, and all these things shall be added to you.

(Matthew 6:33)

If you have moved away from God's standard, you have descended to a level you were never intended to occupy. You probably do not even recognize who you have become, or even more damnable – you don't notice that you have changed!

Think back to your childhood dreams where you saw yourself. Maybe with an excellent career and a wonderful family, is that what you have achieved? Or maybe you are "living your dream". Then the question is, do you have that deep inner peace?

Why not?

Because the more sin entangles you, the less the family resemblance. You will never fulfill God's will until your will is bent towards Him.

IT'S KILLING ME!

...*He was a murderer from the beginning...* (John 8: 44)

Criterion six: **YOU WILL HAVE A DESTRUCTIVE NATURE**. There are some who would rather kill the people who are telling them the truth than change the live they are living. They claim "I don't need you" when one who loves them confronts them with the truth.

They will use harsh words to try to break their spirit so that they will give up on them, because they have already given up on themselves. They would rather kill than change.

...and does not stand in the truth... (John 8: 44)

Criterion seven: **WHEN ONE IS CONSISTENTLY INCONSISTENT IN MATTERS OF TRUTH**. Notice it does not say he does not *know* truth. He is just unstable *in* truth; he cannot stand in it. Many of us know the right thing to do but are as weak as dishwater. We do not know how to stand in what is right and true, so every time something comes up, we are pulled back and forth.

We are told, however,

...that we should no longer be children, tossed to and fro and carried about with every wind of doctrine, by the trickery of men, in the cunning craftiness of deceitful plotting.

(Ephesians 4:14)

Do not let temporary stress or frustrations make you get amnesia. Do not forget what it took to get you out of your mess, because as soon as you start getting lonely, needy or desperate, the thing you asked God to deliver you from will start looking attractive to you again. We tend to enjoy what is comfortable and familiar, because it does not challenge us to change.

Remember,

...the sufferings of this present time are not worthy to be compared with the glory which shall be revealed in us.

(Romans 8:18)

STRETCHING THE TRUTH

When he speaks a lie, he speaks from his own resources, for he is a liar and the father of it.

(John 8:44c)

There are some people who volunteer a lie as quickly as say, "Good Morning". Here in lies criterion number eight: **ONE WHO LIES HABITUALLY**. The thing that makes a lie so damnable is that it has just enough truth in it to make it believable. You have to watch people who pervert truth, who stretch the story to make it more appealing. You can call it embellish, spicing it up, exaggerating or telling it from your own perspective. But no, it is merely a lie.

When you tell God, "I don't want to lie anymore", He will put a check in your spirit when you begin to stretch the truth. It is almost like water going down your windpipe, because it is better to choke on the truth than to breathe freely on a lie. These traits that have been discussed can be used to clear up the questions concerning one's spiritual DNA. Now tell me, "Who's your daddy?"

YOU CAN'T MISS WHAT YOU NEVER HAD

I asked my daughter some years back, "Baby, do you miss North Dakota?" She said "North Dakota? I've never been to North Dakota."

"What about Oklahoma or Iowa?"

"Daddy, I've never been to those places"

My point is you cannot really miss what you have never had.

My daughter can try to conjure feelings about what someone else told her about Oklahoma, North Dakota or Iowa, but she cannot miss those places she has never been. Many lament and cry because they miss their father, when in reality their father was never in their life in the first place.

They are simply allowing someone else's picture of family to cause them to think they missed something. Please understand, I am not minimizing the value of the presence of a father in a child's life. I know that pain all to well. What I *am* saying is, that if one is in a loving and nurturing environment, one parent's absence can be off-set by the community of extended family, be it relatives, church, etc.

You cannot miss what you never had!

If one is not careful, what you are really doing is making the role of those people who stayed with you, who did not leave, seem meaningless. Because you do not appreciate the ones who stayed, or devalue their significance, God will never allow you to reconcile with the ones who are gone.

You must first learn to value those who never left.

LIFE AND DEATH

My mother is eighty-eight years old today. Many years ago, when I was eight years old, my mother decided she was no longer going to allow her children to be abused by their father; my dad. So she picked us up by herself, all six of us and moved on. I was told that there were originally supposed to be eight children in our family, however. My mother was pregnant just before and just after I was born, but due to complication with the pregnancies, those babies died.

Although I did not know it at the time, I was born between deaths. God protected me from the death that surrounded me. Likewise, there are situations you are not even aware of that happened before you and after you but yet did not come near you, because God protected you from them.

Thank God you survived.

DON'T OPEN THE DOOR

I call my mother a saint because all those years after her departure, she never divorced. She was young enough to still have sexual desires, but I never knew of my mother in a relationship with anyone other than my father. She made the welfare of her children her highest priority, and that act has blessed us to this day.

Whether your children see what you do or not, the spirit of what you are doing will be over your child. Those children came through your womb, and therefore you become the open door for any spirit, yours or anyone else's, who you invite into your life. Wherever you went, wherever you go even now that they are grown, that door is open for those spirits to come upon your children.

Those innocent virgin spirits are wide open to every demon that you connect with. Do not expose them!

WHAT SON IS NOT DISCIPLINED?

But as many as received Him, to them He gave the right to become children of God, to those who believe in His name:

(John 1:12)

If you are going to call God your Father, you must receive Him and believe Him.

Hebrews 12:7 adds,

If you endure chastening, God deals with you as with sons; for what son is there whom a father does not chasten?

When you cannot handle God's discipline, you are calling yourself illegitimate, a bastard. There are some who want to run from the chastisement of their "Father".

But you ought to love a father who loves you enough to discipline you. You ought to love anyone who watches your life or cares enough to say "That's not what you need to be doing".

You do not need a *yes man* or a flunky; you need someone who loves you enough to say, "I am willing to jeopardize our relationship. There is more to you than this. You are living beneath your potential."

Although you may not want to hear it today, there will come a day when you are sitting in the pigsty of life and you will be glad to remember that you have a father who believed in you and loved you enough to let you go – not just someone who has you for a few weeks during summertime and buys you new clothing or tennis shoes.

You want somebody who prays for you and is an example of what you ought to be. Someone you can look to with pride and say, "That's my father".

"15 Then he went and joined himself to a citizen of that country, and he sent him into his fields to feed swine. 16 And he would gladly have filled his stomach with the pods that the swine ate, and no one gave him anything.

[17] *'But when he came to himself, he said, 'How many of my father's hired servants have bread enough and to spare, and I perish with hunger!* [18] *I will arise and go to my father…"*

(Luke 15:15-18a)

Sitting in a pigsty is not nearly so bad if you know you have a family, a father, to go home to.

LOOK IN THE MIRROR

How can we restore our true family resemblance? By accepting the discipline of our Father and obeying His Word.

Scripture explains,

How can a young man cleanse his way? By taking heed according to Your Word.

(Psalm 119:9)

We desperately need the washing of the water of the word so that we may accurately reflect the image of our true Father. Our prayer needs to be that of David in Psalm 51.

PRAYER POINT

Father! Transform me to the image of Your Dear Son. In Jesus' Mighty Name, Amen!

SCRIPTURE REFERENCE:

Colossians 1:9-23

Chapter Four

When Your Faith is Weak

DEALING WITH THE DEVIL

And the Lord said, "Simon, Simon! Indeed, Satan has asked for you, that he may sift you as wheat. 32 *But I have prayed for you, that your faith should not fail; and when you have returned to Me, strengthen your brethren."*

(Luke 22:31-32)

When the conversation in this passage took place, all of the disciples had been in the upper room for the Last Supper. They had all partaken of Jesus' body and His blood, as it were. They had questioned Him concerning what was about to take place, and they had argued about who was going to be the greatest, and who was going to sit on one side or other of His throne.

Two of them, brothers, even had the audacity to have their mother ask for special privileges for her two boys. It was on the heels of all this that Jesus then turned and spoke to one person in particular. Although He was on His way to fulfill His own destiny, He suddenly stopped to talk to Peter about his destiny.

Interestingly, Jesus did not call him by his post-declaration name, Peter, the name he was called after he made the confession; *Thou art the Christ, the son of the Living God* (Matthew 16:16).

Instead He called him by his pre-revelation name, Simon, and even said it twice, implying the severity of the term.

Jesus wanted to make it abundantly clear that rather than addressing the man who was a result of revelation, He was speaking to who Peter was when he was in his pre-revelation state.

JUST AN AVERAGE JOE

Why would Satan specifically single out Simon, rather than any of the other disciples, especially Judas, whom he had already begun utilizing? It is because those who are going to do great things for the Kingdom come under Satan's scrutiny.

So those of you who want to be normal, who want to be average, who want to settle for mediocrity, you will not really have to worry too much about the devil. Satan does not want those who have nothing to offer. Daniel 1:3-4 reports that Nebuchadnezzar, King of Babylon, wanted those young people who were intelligent, good looking and without blemish to be taught the Chaldean language and given positions of authority so he took those who were qualified into bondage.

Likewise, our enemy does not want the junk, the mess, and the throwaways in life. He wants the best that life has to offer. He wants those who have great minds and can fly through college without thinking. He wants the ones who can do Microsoft a favor. He wants the ones who have the ability to impact the world.

The devil is looking for those who have something to offer, not the ones who are trying to be involved in every form of addictive lifestyle and promiscuity. Not the ones who are content to stand on the corner and sell themselves.

He does use the ones who choose to stand on the corner, however, to *pull down* those who will impact their world.

I'LL TAKE THAT ONE

If you know that God is going to use you, you must also be aware that Satan has already sought permission to try to thwart you. If on the other hand, you are expecting to have everything you want in life, to have everyone love you, you will most certainly *not* be doing great things for the Kingdom.

Because in order to get the best of heaven, you will be required to go through hell. Just saying, "I love Jesus" is not enough. II Timothy 2:12 teaches, those who "suffer with Him will also reign with Him". You will not receive a crown if you do not pick up a cross; there is no resurrection without a crucifixion. In order for you to get what God has for you, something has to die.

THE WHEAT AND THE WEEDS

Satan asked for Peter specifically, not because he wanted Peter per se', but because he wanted to separate him from his destiny, "that he may sift him as wheat". The concept of sifting wheat comes from ancient times.

After they had taken sickles and cut the wheat, what remained was wheat and tares (weeds) mixed together. So they would throw the mixture up in the air while sweeping side to side with the sharp sickle as it fell to the ground.

Then they would gather it all up and put it in a pan with a screen. The screen's holes were so small, that only the wheat (good for flour) would fall through. Any tares, pebbles or bugs were left on top of the screen.

Literally the passage is saying that the devil wants to throw you up in the air, to cut you, to separate you from everything that you thought you were or was of value.

If it seems like you have been stuck with sharp daggers and it looks like all the people you relied upon are pulling away, there is a sifting going on. Only that which is good for produce is going to make it through.

YOU GET RIGHT BACK UP AGAIN

There are certain reasons that the devil wants you, although there are other people who may be in the same place as you whom he is not concerned about.

Why Peter?

It was Peter who said, "I'll go all the way". It was Peter who was always speaking up. It was Peter who was making promises, stepping out in faith, walking on water.

The devil said "I may not know about Pentecost coming because I don't know the future, but when I look at your past, I see you have a habit of making promises to God, and when you mess up, you at least have the sense to come back and try again".

If the devil sees something in you that says you will try again, he will come after you. He does not care about the ones who give up and quit every time life gets difficult. He wants the ones who mess up, get back up and say, "Lord, if You dust me off and smack me on my rump, I'll get back into the game again".

Proverbs 24:16 declares:

...a righteous man may fall seven times and rise again, but the wicked shall fall by calamity.

It is not as important that you fall. What is important is that you get back up again!

Remember,

It is good for me that I have been afflicted, that I may learn Your statutes.

(Psalm 119:71)

THE MIDDLEMAN

Here is our hope:

...But I have prayed for you, that your faith should not fail; and when you have returned to Me, strengthen your brethren.

(Luke 22:32)

The devil has been asking for you, but while he was asking, Jesus was praying. It is a wonderful thing to know that when nobody else is thinking about you, the Lord is praying for you.

...Since He always lives to make intercession for them.

(Hebrews 7:25)

Jesus is the propitiation, the go between, the middleman. He stands before the Father and says, "Give them another chance for My sake".

And if Jesus is praying that your faith does not fail, then you ought to be praying that as well. The Word tells us we are to have the same mind as that which is in Christ Jesus (Philippians 2:5). In other words, do not merely pray and ask Him for the job you want; pray that you have faith to trust Him for whatever He is going to give you.

LIMITED VISION

In His prayer for Peter, Jesus revealed the real issue that is at stake; what the enemy is out to do, no matter what area he meddles in, is to make you forfeit your faith.

Scripture tells us,

Now faith is the substance of things hoped for, the evidence of things not seen.

(Hebrews 11:1)

In other words, what you want that is visible has its origin in an invisible realm. What you really want is not where you can see it, because what you can see is temporary. What you cannot see is permanent. What you can see is based on your limited vision, but there is no limit to what you cannot see.

If the enemy convinces you to forfeit your faith, he then makes you focus on what you can see, instead of focusing on what you cannot see, so that you will always live a limited life and never live what Jesus said in John 10:10b:

I have come that they may have life, and that they may have it more abundantly.

MIGHTY HARD TO PLEASE

The devil also attacks your faith because,

But without faith it is impossible to please Him.

(Hebrews 11:6a)

God is not moved by anything if you do not have faith – which means you can holler, cry, spit or cuss and God will not move.

You can tithe, jump up and down, throw money on the altar and still, God will not move.

Why? Because unless you are moved by faith, you cannot move God. It does not matter how many scriptures you quote, if you do not have faith to believe what you are saying, then none of what you have done was for God, it was for your flesh. And if it was not motivated by faith, then God was not moved by it.

But let him ask in faith, with no doubting, for he who doubts is like a wave of the sea driven and tossed by the wind. [7]For let not that man suppose that he will receive anything from the Lord.

(James 1:6-7)

In other words, you cannot have expectation without faith.

DO YOU HAVE TOO MUCH *SENSE*?

The struggle is that we live in a visible world, and are a sense-oriented people; we rely on our smell, our touch, our hearing, and our taste. We are sense-oriented and living in a world that is sense-ual. And no, I do not mean *sexual*, although that is generally true; I mean *sensual*, sense oriented.

In his wisdom, the devil messes with what you can see to make you doubt what you cannot see. The truth of the matter is, he is really not trying to get your job, your family or your finances.

What he is doing is touching what he knows you recognize as blessings, or what you associate with God being good. You praise the Lord if everything is right with your family, you shout if God gives you the car.

You thank him if you get the loan. The enemy is trying to make you start equating the goodness of God to the sensual things that happen in life.

But you must understand and believe that God is good even if your house does not get the breakthrough, even if your children are not yet delivered or even if you get fired.

NO MATTER HOW LONG IT TAKES

…*The just shall live by his faith* (Habakkuk 2:4)

and

we walk by faith, not by sight (2 Corinthians 5:7).

So what the enemy tries to do by attacking your faith is hinder your walk, make you settle for mediocrity and cease to want to move. His goal is to *distract* you from obtaining what you believe God for. Many people make the mistake of blaming God for what they did not continue to believe. *Faith is not faith if it is not consistent.*

You believe God for a job by next Friday. But if after Friday, you think God let you down, you never really believed Him for Friday, because faith has got to be consistent.

You have to believe God no matter how long it takes.

TRAMPOLINE FAITH

Then one of the crowd answered and said, "Teacher, I brought You my son, who has a mute spirit. [18]And wherever it seizes him, it throws him down; he foams at the mouth, gnashes his teeth, and becomes rigid. So I spoke to Your disciples, that they should cast it out, but they could not." [19]He answered him and said, "O faithless generation, how long shall I be with you? How long shall I bear with you? Bring him to Me." [20]Then they brought him to Him. And when he saw Him, immediately the spirit convulsed him, and he fell on the ground and wallowed, foaming at the mouth. [21]So He asked his father, How long has this been happening to him?"And he said, "From childhood. [22]And often he has thrown him both into the fire and into the water to destroy him. But if You can do anything, have compassion on us and help us." [23]*Jesus said to him, "If you can believe, all things are possible to him who believes."* 24*Immediately the father of the child cried out and said with tears, "Lord, I believe; help my unbelief!"*

(Mark 9:17-24)

Many people over the years have made the mistake of teaching about the father or the boy in this passage above. The truth of the matter, however, is this story is really not about the boy or the father, but the boy and the father bring out the real point of the text: *faith*, if it is anything, ought to be a trampoline.

Remember, Romans 12:3:

...God has dealt to each one a measure of faith

So the issue is not a lack of faith, but its ability to bounce back after disappointments. Contained within this story are descriptions of situations which challenge the strength and elasticity of our faith.

Despite the circumstances we find our self in, we must be always able, through faith, to bounce back on to our feet. Why? Because we as believers ought not be moved by what we have seen or by what has happened.

We understand that happiness is based on happenings; whereas our joy is based on our knowledge of God's Word and His will for us, His children.

So many people are miserable because they are basing their happiness on what they have or on what is happening in their lives. I do not waste time with that! I have the joy of the Lord as my strength. I have trampoline faith.

BUILDING YOUR STRENGTH

I must confess, however, that my faith is still a bit weak in some areas. I could attempt to downplay the problem, after all, my faith is strong in some areas and weak in just a few, but I have learned that weak faith, just like any type of disease, will eventually affect every other area.

One cannot claim victory in one area while ignoring another, because if you are not careful, you will wind up spending more time focusing on what you are good at and never dealing with that you are bad at.

So if our faith does not always have the strength it is supposed to have, what then are the things that challenge out faith? The continuation of this story bears out various challenges.

IT'S ALL IN THE FAMILY

Teacher, I brought You my son, possessed with a spirit which makes him mute.

(Mark 9:17)

The first challenge is **THE DIFFICULTY OF DEALING WITH YOUR OWN FAMILY**. It is certainly not difficult to pray for other people, their children, their spouses, and their jobs. But when issues arise in your own family, suddenly you cannot find the faith to pray, because you struggle to believe.

If you confess, *as far as me and my house, we will serve the Lord* (Joshua 24:15) and you saw God promise that your whole house would be saved, and that no sickness would come near your dwelling, the enemy will be sure to touch that area so that you will be distracted from what you have been believing God for.

It is hard for one, I must admit, to have faith for what seemingly touches your own world. You may be able to believe for everybody else's child to get a breakthrough, but when you look at your own child acting out, all of a sudden your faith is under attack.

But if you cannot look at that crack-addicted son and see him getting back up, you do not have trampoline faith.

WORSE AND WORSE

The second challenge to your faith occurs when **YOUR PROBLEMS CONTINUE TO ESCALATE WHILE YOU ARE BELIEVING**.

[18]*And wherever it seizes him, it throws him down; he foams at the mouth, gnashes his teeth, and becomes rigid... ...*[20]*the spirit convulsed him, and he fell on the ground and wallowed, foaming at the mouth...* [22]*And often he has thrown him both into the fire and into the water to destroy him.*

(Mark 9:18a, 20b, 22a)

This boy's problem started out one way – falling down, gnashing his teeth; then increased to convulsions, wallowing, falling into fire and water. In your life as well, the enemy will continue touching situations to make them appear worse and worse, so that you will start focusing on what you can see and give up on what you cannot see. It is then that the enemy will cause you to say, "What is the use?"

Instead you must be able to say,

Though He slay me, yet will I trust Him. (Job 13:15a)

When you feel a lump and lay hands on it, believing God, and it gets bigger; when you say you are healed but the next thing you know, they are taking you under the knife – your faith is shaken.

This is the devil's intent – he wants you to doubt the Great Physician. You believed God, yet it looks like your healing has not come. If the enemy can get you doubting Him now, when you are sick, then you will not believe Him down the road when something greater comes up.

OH FAITHLESS GENERATION

O faithless generation, how long shall I bear with you?

(Mark 9:19)

The real issue in this passage is not about the son or the father; it is about the generation in which they were living. What do you do when no one in your peer group has faith for what you have been believing God for?

What happens when you are surrounded by a generation of people who have no faith for finishing school, for staying pure, for staying chaste; a generation of people who see no need for prayer, who all stay out late, where nobody is trying to live holy unto God?

The generation that we live in, especially in America, is cursed – it is the first generation where people's grandparents have never met God because the grandparents are only 40 years old.

HELP ME, CHURCH!

So I spoke to Your disciples, that they should cast it out, but they could not.

Mark 9:18b)

Another challenge to your faith is **WHEN GOING TO CHURCH DOES NOT SEEM TO HELP**.

Perhaps you are struggling with a certain sin, you come to church and instead of deliverance, you end up connecting with someone wrapped up in the same sin. Maybe your fall came through a brother or sister in church who was supposed to be praying for you but who *preyed* on you instead.

Perhaps you keep telling your fellow brethren what you are facing is not merely a problem but a spirit, but no one has an answer. Your prayer partner will not pray, your intercessor will not intercede. It is difficult when the "church" does not seem to have the answer to your situation.

There are some issues that the church has not addressed and others that she ignores. But please, do not judge Jesus by the church! He still admonishes, *Bring it to Me.*

HOW DID THAT GET THERE?

So He asked his father, "How long has this been happening to him?" And he said, "From childhood.

(Mark 9:21)

The implication here is that this was not a little boy but a grown man, and something in his childhood had allowed the enemy access to his life. Even though he is older, the open door in his childhood is still affecting him. *When something has been in your life for so long that you cannot even pinpoint when it started, it is hard to have faith for a victory.*

Jesus made this man go back down memory lane, uncovering the years and weeks and days, to pinpoint when the boy started acting that way. Similarly, you have some work to do. You need to go back over your past and try to figure out where you lost your faith. When did you give up on your future? When did you decide you could not live a holy life?

Many people will never pinpoint the beginning because they are too lazy to do the work; others are merely too timid.

But no one else can go back in your life and figure out what happened; only you know why you do what you do. In addition, it is important that you discover the times and seasons of your problem. Every Sunday, right after service, you jump right into something from which you just prayed for deliverance. Friday night, Saturday night, there's an *itch* to do something; on payday, every holiday, around your birthday.

You must be able to *discern the times*! I will discuss the power of timing in chapters seven, eight and eleven.

PRAYER POINT

Father! Let my confidence and trust be in You and You alone! In Jesus' Mighty Name, Amen!

SCRIPTURE REFERENCE:

Psalm 20: 7-8

Chapter Five

Finding the Remedy

BRING IT TO JESUS

O faithless generation, how long shall I be with you? How long shall I bear with you? ***Bring him to Me****.*

(Mark 9: 19)

Whatever it is that has caused your faith to be weak, you must release it to Jesus. He says, "Bring it to Me. It started in childhood? Fine, bring me your childhood problem. Bring me your molestation.

Bring me your abandonment. Bring me the fact that they locked you in the closet and now you have fear of darkness. I don't care how old it is, bring it to me. Bring me all the things that make you think that I am an absentee God."

Whatever issues or unreconciled differences you have not dealt with from your childhood, as it relates to authority or parental problems, is one of the main reasons you cannot trust God as your Heavenly Father when you are an adult. If you had an earthly father who abandoned you, you cannot believe that our Heavenly Father is going to stay.

JUST LET IT GO

Anything you have been holding on to, all the behaviors that have been your defense, need to be dealt with. You hold onto some things because they make people keep their distance. You hold onto other things because they give you a sense of security. Some things you hold unto because you are afraid of being alone, because if you are ever by yourself, you have to deal with yourself.

So you run over to friends' houses and always want to ride in their car, because you know if you are in your room by yourself, in your car by yourself, in your cubicle by yourself, you will have to deal with yourself – and then you cannot blame anyone else for who you are. For you see, the one person that you cannot lie to about you is *you*.

EXTREME UNBALANCE

And often he has thrown him both into the fire and into the water to destroy him.

(Mark 9:24a)

This was a boy whose life was full of extremes; one second in fire, the next second in the water. His life had never had balance. If the boy could simply have put the fire and the water together, he could have had a warm comfortable bath. But he had no balance in his life. Likewise, many people are extremists, either running hot or cold, never balanced in between; either hot for the devil or cold towards God.

Perhaps you have no balance in your life. You are either heavy for God or not for God at all. You are living like you love Jesus or living like you are the devil's pal. Jesus wants you to get some balance. But balance requires discipline.

If you *are not disciplined*, you will have *to be disciplined.* God cannot reward you when are not balanced.

I MADE A MESS!

But if You can do anything, have compassion on us and help us.

(Mark 9:22b)

Not only must you release your problems to Jesus, you also have to admit to Him and to yourself that you cannot resolve issues on your own. You must stop trying to act as if you know how to get yourself together, because all you are really doing through all your fleshy effort is driving yourself farther away from Him.

Some years ago, there was a song, written by the late Bishop Walter Hawkins, which said, "No one knows like I know how hard I've tried and still made a mess of my life." However, it is not enough to simply admit that you do not know how to help yourself.

You have to stop *trying* to help yourself. It is a bad thing when you are doing everything you know how to do and your life is not getting any better. What is worse is when you will not stop trying, even though you *know* you are making a bigger mess of your life. If no one can speak into your life, no one can reason with you, there is something wrong.

You are making a mess of your life and do not know how to stop. Your secular humanistic mindset, your wealth, your degrees, your physical beauty and strength give you a false sense of control. But you need to admit that you truly do not know what you are doing.

HOLLER FOR HELP

Lord, I believe; help my unbelief. (Mark 9: 24b)

You may have enough faith to say you believe, but the truth of the matter is, you need more than belief, you now need help. If you really want to get out of the mess that you are in, you must drop your pride. Drop your image. Forget about what people are saying about you. Throw your head back, open your mouth and simply shout, "Help!"

Until you holler for help, you have fooled yourself into believing that you are doing all you are *supposed* to do to get your deliverance, therefore you will never ask for help. But if you are tired of living like you are living, going around the same mountain over and over again, you must be willing to say, "I don't care how you do it. Lord, help my unbelief"

If you already knew what to do, or if you already knew the way out, then why haven't you taken it? The fact that you are not out of it yet means you must stop trying to have control over how you are delivered and just open your mouth.

THERE IS NO MIDDLE GROUND

And he led Him up and showed Him all the kingdoms of the world in a moment of time. 6And the devil said to Him, "I will give You all this domain and its glory; for it has been handed over to me, and I give it to whomever I wish.

(Luke 4:5-6, NASB)

Why do you think the devil wants your house when he has all the kingdoms of the world? Why does he want your job? Those are not what he is after. He is after whatever you are after, so he can get *you.*

He gets you by disrupting the serenity of your house, your job, etc., until you are so mad at God that you will not go to Him. Understand, you do not have to go to the devil for him to have you; all you have to do is stop going to God. There is no middle ground.

If you are not for God, you are against Him. Whether you say "I am anti-Christian" or you simply have not accepted Him yet, you are against Him – which means you are automatically in the hand of the enemy. You must understand *there is no middle ground.* You cannot straddle the fence. You are either going after God with faith or you will be running from Him in fear.

IGNORANCE IS NO EXCUSE

My people are destroyed for lack of knowledge. Because you have rejected knowledge, I also will reject you from being priest for Me; because you have forgotten the law of your God, I also will forget your children.

(Hosea 4:6)

Ignorance is an invitation to demonic activity; contrary to popular belief, what you don't know *will* kill you. God never intended for you and I as believers to live lives that are despondent, depressed, depleted and/or defeated. Yet many congregations are populated by individuals who live hopeless, hapless and helpless lives. Fear and poverty reside where faith and power are supposed to abide.

It is not because of a lack of "church" – we have mastered church. We know how to jump, how to run, how to speak in tongues. We know how to do everything concerning Pentecost, but because there is no application of what we shouted about once leaving the building, many are still struggling. We have all the right CDs, and have read every book. We have been to every conference and every seminar.

We are doing everything that we can think of and yet we are not experiencing any long term victory. You can repeat sermons and you know where all the essential Scriptures are found. Yet when it comes to your own life, you do not have victory.

Why is that?

Because you will not stay true to the information that you have received.

JUST DO IT

The Bible commands:

But be doers of the word, and not hearers only, deceiving yourselves.

(James 1:22)

In other words, if you do not apply what you have been instructed in, it has not really made an impression on your life. The proof of whether a thing is real or not to you is: do you live it out? You may *read* the Word and *hear* the Word and *quote* the Word, but if you are living contrary *to* the Word, then your *lifestyle* is more real to you than the Word you quote.

It only becomes real to you when you put it into action and it works for you. It is not real or relevant Word simply because it is preached and gets results in other people's lives. It is real and relevant when you try it for yourself, live it in your own life, and then are able to say "I know in whom I believe". You cannot say you know in whom you believe if you have not believed enough to live for who you know!

Quoting the Word may make it true in content but not true in context. It is true and you heard it but it is not true in the application in your own life. You have to try it and prove it for yourself.

THE WRONG IMPRESSION

Simply to say that you have heard the Word means nothing if you don't apply it – without application, you will have the impression that you know the truth even though it is not real for you. Many are deceived. You have been hearing and hearing the Word until you know it, and before the pastor starts preaching, you say, "I know what he's going to say".

Yes, but if you are not living it, knowing it puts you under bondage of self deception. The enemy will give you the impression that you know the truth, and you will walk into situations over which you think you have victory but because you have never lived that truth, you will be defeated.

This is why there are many individuals in the church today who are just as undisciplined and inconsistent and in bondage as the ones who are in the world. These individuals mistakenly thought that being in church got conviction into them. They thought that shouting when somebody else shouted meant they were filled with the Holy Ghost.

They thought that being around people who are anointed meant that they were anointed. So they started walking into places thinking they could get out, but they did not have the power that they thought they had. Further, if the wisdom of the Word had been present, they would have simply "avoided" some places in the first place!

It is a bad thing to get into the middle of something and think that you can call on God but He does not answer you because you have not established a relationship with Him.

DIRE STRAITS

There are more church people in bondage, more church people in dire straits, more church people lying on psychologists' couches, more church people having bouts with despair and suicide, that there is not a difference between those in church and those in the world. There are more people in the church who are trying to get a hit of crack, find some weed, and do anything to try to deal with the pressure of life than we have seen in any other time.

Whatever happened to:

...these signs will follow those who believe: In My name they will cast out demons; they will speak with new tongues.

(Mark 16:17)

Whatever happened to:

...in all these things we are more than conquerors through Him who loved us. [38]*For I am persuaded that neither death nor life, nor angels nor principalities nor powers, nor things present nor things to come,* [39]*nor height nor depth, nor any other created thing, shall be able to separate us from the love of God which is in Christ Jesus our Lord.*

(Romans 8:37-39)

Whatever happened to:

I can do all things through Christ who strengthens me.

(Philippians 4:13)

THE VICTIM MENTALITY

The saints being under attack is not the problem; that is expected. The problem is, far too many saints are losing battles that they should have been winning. Even worse, they are losing battles they should not be fighting!

They are becoming victims of the very things that they should be victorious over. And while they are victims, they also become hindrances. How so? The ones they are supposed to be helping, sadly, they become the very ones that the devil uses the most to fragment the body of Christ and bring about division and schisms.

Instead of them showing these new disciples how to live in holiness, they pull them into a greater mess. When you have not dealt with your demon, you have no ability to help others change. You either leave them as they are, or make them worse than they were before they ever met you.

But woe to you, scribes and Pharisees, hypocrites! For you shut up the kingdom of heaven against men; for you neither go in yourselves, nor do you allow those who are entering to go in. 14 *Woe to you, scribes and Pharisees, hypocrites! For you devour widows' houses, and for a pretense make long prayers. Therefore you will receive greater condemnation.* 15 *Woe to you, scribes and Pharisees, hypocrites! For you travel land and sea to win one proselyte, and when he is won, you make him twice as much a son of hell as yourselves.*

(Matthew 23:13-15)

Who have you come in contact with? Were they any better when you walked out of their lives? Or were they deeper in their sin?

The good news is you *can* lead a victorious life, you *can* strengthen your brothers and sister – once you identify, expose and deal with your demon.

PRAYER POINT

Father! Bring balance to my life so that I can become an asset and not a liability to Your Kingdom. In Jesus' Mighty Name, Amen!

SCRIPTURE REFERENCE:

Proverbs 11:1

Section 2

EXPOSING THE ADVERSARY

Chapter Six

Exposing Your Demons

EXPRESS YOURSELF!

Then one of the crowd answered and said, "Teacher, I brought You my son, who has a mute spirit. [18]*And wherever it seizes him, it throws him down; he foams at the mouth, gnashes his teeth, and becomes rigid. So I spoke to Your disciples, that they should cast it out, but they could not."* [28]*And when He had come into the house, His disciples asked Him privately, "Why could we not cast it out?"* [29]*So He said to them, "This kind can come out by nothing but prayer and fasting."*

(Mark 9:17-18, 28-29)

This man has a child, but the problem is the child has a demon. Notice the father does not try to pretend that the child has an "issue". He says outright that his child has a spirit. He does not try to minimize the nature of his son's problem. He does not blame it on society or relegate it to an episode in his life. He goes to the root. He exposes the source. Its origin is spiritual, manifesting in the natural.

The first thing the father noticed is the spirit causes his son to be mute. **IT IS A SPIRIT THAT WILL NOT LET THAT SON EXPRESS HIMSELF**. People are going to express what they are feeling either by what they say or by what they do.

When there is a spirit that will not let an individual say what he feels, he is then *forced* to act out of what he feels. What is it that causes a child to come into a certain age of their life and then suddenly not be able to speak to his mother or father?

It is a spirit.

Your mother pushed you out of her womb; you should be able to talk to her. A good father works to keep you clothed, sheltered and provided for; he will not understand if you cannot speak to him. If you are not able to express yourself, to articulate what you are feeling, there maybe a spirit, an unseen agent residing in the deeper region of one's being, influencing you to act this way.

DON'T JUST TALK ABOUT IT

So I spoke to Your disciples, that they should cast it out, but they could not."

(Mark 9: 18b)

The father brought his demon-possessed son to the disciples, the leadership of the church. What did the leadership do? *They talked about it.* All they did was talk about it.

The leadership talked about it, but the demon did not come out. The problem with the church today is that everyone wants counseling; everyone wants to talk about their problems. But there are some things you do not need counseling for; rather, you need deliverance. You cannot keep on pacifying yourself and pretending that you can stop when you want to. You must acknowledge that you need help. Your problem is not communication. *You need the unlawful agent of the devil to be cast out of your life, your affairs and your family*!

THE NAME BUT NOT THE NATURE

And when He had come into the house, His disciples asked Him privately, "Why could we not cast it out?"

(Mark 9:28)

The disciples had a public embarrassment but wanted to talk about it privately. In the same way, most of us try to have our public dirt and then want private deliverance. Think of how we make Jesus look to the world! We carry His name but we do not have His nature. We say He is our Father but we do not have His power. The man brought his son to the disciples because they have been with Jesus. They were not some young immature whippersnappers; they had been handpicked by Jesus.

He had personally chosen these men and then gave them daily hands-on, on-the-job training so they could watch what He did and imitate Him. He trained them, gave them free food, paid their taxes, did everything; and in return, they could offer nothing to His program when it came to the heavy issue of demons. Perhaps you went to church leadership and told them what you struggled with, and they prayed about your struggle.

However, the next thing you knew, you were doing the same thing in church that you were doing in the world. Praying without power is not going to solve anything. These were handpicked disciples with no real ability to deal with the issues. They could talk, they could communicate, but they could not cast out the evil spirit. It is no good when you can talk the talk, but when it comes to the time to back up your talk with a lifestyle, you cannot walk the walk!

DO WHAT YOU HAVE TO DO

Why could they not cast this demon out of the boy? It was not a whole crowd of people; it was one man's son, and the father was giving them permission to do whatever they had to do. In some situations, the parents do not want to admit that they have failed, they do not want anyone else to minster to their children.

But here is a willing father, saying, "I recognize I have done all I can do. It is not my fault that my child is acting like this. I raised him right. If he is acting like this and there is no resemblance to me, there is a spirit in there somewhere"

WHAT KIND IS THIS?

This kind can come out by nothing but prayer and fasting.

(Mark 9:29)

Now, because the text says, this *kind*, it implies that there is more than one kind of demon. Not just various kinds but various types. "This kind" also implies that there are various amounts of demons. Mark 5:9 tells us the man on the Coast of the Gadarenes had "legions" of demons in him. According to Mathew 12: 43-45,

When an unclean spirit goes out of a man, he goes through dry places, seeking rest, and finds none. 44Then he says, 'I will return to my house from which I came.' And when he comes, he finds it empty, swept, and put in order. 45Then he goes and takes with him seven other spirits more wicked than himself, and they enter and dwell there; and the last state of that man is worse than the first. So shall it also be with this wicked generation.

If there are seven new spirits plus the original one, there must be at least eight different kinds, or types, or varieties.

Further, Ephesians 6:12 describes different *levels* of spirits:

For we do not wrestle against flesh and blood, but against principalities, against powers, against the rulers of the darkness of this age, against spiritual hosts of wickedness in the heavenly places.

IS IT A DUCK?

So what kind of demon was this? You can tell the kind of demon by his actions and activities. This passage contains several characteristics that will expose this particular demon, but will also help you identify the ones which you are struggling with. I want you to be able to look at this and say, "I see this one in me." Now, I am not saying that you have a demon necessarily, but if it looks like a duck and walks like a duck, if it has a bill, it quacks and it is yellow, it is probably a duck. Likewise, if you note several of these traits in you, or someone you care about, you may want to seek help from a genuine man or woman of God for assistance.

DON'T UNDERESTIMATE THE DEVIL

And He asked the scribes, "What are you discussing with them?"

(Mark 9:16)

The first reason they could not cast out this spirit is because **THEY UNDERESTIMATED THE TYPE OF DEMON THEY WERE DEALING WITH**. They thought they were dealing with a demon they could just command to come out. According to 2 Corinthians 2:11, you should not be ignorant of the devil's devices. He gets an advantage when you do not know certain things. Many do not want to read His word, come to Bible study, or listen to sound teaching; they simply want to talk about why they are struggling.

But if you would simply apply what is available, you would have victory where you are currently having defeat. Be aware. Do not underestimate the type of demon you are dealing with, because *that* demon is not going to let you go without a fight. You are a choice item if you have forfeited your anointing just to get into whatever the devil had to offer.

Now, you do not even have the ability to trust your anointing. Why? Because once you have forfeited it to get into the mess with the devil, he has convinced you that you do not have a right to pray, to call on God, or to live holy. You need to know what kind of demon you are dealing with. What kind of demon has perverted *your* mind?

OUT OF CONTROL

And wherever it seizes him, it throws him down; he foams at the mouth, gnashes his teeth, and becomes rigid.

(Mark 9:18a)

This demon, when it has control, starts something and then makes it looks like it was your idea because you are the one finishing it. This is a spirit that will put you up to something, and then when everything starts going bad, will step back and make it look like it was your idea, your agenda, and then make you think you have to get yourself out of it.

Whenever you have to have control, there could be a strong hold. This spirit will make you think you are what you do. But what it really does is give you enough control to set yourself up, just not enough to get yourself out.

If the Holy Ghost can move through you, then the *unholy* ghost can too.

This demon seizes him, and throws him down. In response the boy foams at the mouth, grinds and gnashes his teeth and then becomes rigid. *This* demon ***TRIES TO CONTROL THE OPERATION OF YOUR FLESH.***

"I can't stop, I can't help myself. I'm too into him. I'm too into her." That is a spirit controlling your flesh.

"I'll never do this again", but the next thing you know, you are doing the *same* thing again; different person, same spirit.

"I'm a night person. I just can't sleep before five a.m." Did you know all of the greatest sins take place at that time? What are you getting into between ten and five? Are you doing anything worthwhile? You maybe opening the door for more spirits to enter in. Daddy G.O. says that we should use that time to '*fight*' in prayer during the night, so that we can have victory during the day!

HE CAN'T GET ANY RESPECT

Then they brought him to Him. And when he saw Him, immediately the spirit convulsed him, and he fell on the ground and wallowed, foaming at the mouth.

(Mark 9:20)

Another characteristic of this demon is that ***IT HAS NO RESPECT FOR THE PRESENCE OF JESUS.*** When this demon got in the presence of Jesus, he started showing off. He threw the man down, made him wallow in the dirt with no respect for himself or the presence of Jesus. Likewise, when you have no regard for the things of God or the place of God, you have an evil spirit manipulating you.

Whether it be using the Lords name in a profane way, denying His deity, or taking your body (His temple) into immoral or gross perversions, these acts prove the presence and influence of demonic activity. Sadly, there is more flesh on parade in the church today than there is in a club. How dare you go to sleep in church and stay awake in a movie?

While the presence of the Lord is moving and people are getting breakthroughs, you can find some in church are checking their pocketbook. That is not regard for the presence of God. How dare you show up for church late (if at all) and enter as if you are the "star of the show"? How can you decide that you are coming for the most important part, as if you know what is best for you? You need to develop a positive attitude toward the church. You must treat the house of God, His Presence, with reverence and awe.

ACCEPTING ALL AGES

So He asked his father, "How long has this been happening to him?" And he said, "From childhood."

(Mark 9:21)

This is a demon which ***HAS NO AGE REQUIREMENTS***. He will get into your baby, just as easily as he will get into your husband. He will make your two-year-old spit and slap you in the face, just like he will make a grown man punch you in the mouth. He is a demon that has no age requirement, which means that *everyone is open game to him.*

He does not care whether he is trying to kill an infant before he has a chance to get into life, or whether he gets into an older person who has been with God for a long time, causing her to suddenly act like she does not even know who God is. Every age is a prime candidate for this kind of demon.

It does not matter that he has not been with you forever; he can make your life so miserable until it feels like you have never had a good day. The devil is very wise. What he tries to do today is the same thing he did in the Garden of Eden. He tries to get inside of what God loves so that God will face a very hard decision.

He tried to get inside of Adam so that God would either have to ignore Adam's sin because He loved him so, or hate sin so much that He had to kill Adam. That is what the devil tries to do.

He tries to get inside of you, the people that God loves, so that God will have to kill you. But much to the enemy's chagrin, God will neither smile on sin nor kill us. Instead, He put sin on Himself and died on the cross. That way, He dealt with sin and the devil at the same time. Hence, all we need now do is accept Christ as our personal Lord and Savior, and the finished work of Calvary becomes the doormat to our deliverance and eternal destiny!

HEADING FOR DESTRUCTION

This is also a demon ***BENT ON SELF DESTRUCTION.***

And often he has thrown him both into the fire and into the water to destroy him.

(Mark 9:22a)

This demon that these disciples cannot cast out would not be satisfied until it destroyed the man. The devil is not trying to hurt you, maim you, take your job, take your husband, take your wife or merely mess up your kids…*he is trying to destroy you.*

Be sober, be vigilant; because your adversary the devil walks about like a roaring lion, seeking whom he may devour.

(1 Peter 5:8)

He wants to devour you. He does not want there to be any trace of you, your integrity, your character, or of anything in you that shows any good. He wants to kill your ability to influence others. He is bent on your destruction.

He wants you so conditioned to defeat that even when you know something is not good for you, you still either cannot or will not stop. All you have to do is stay out of certain environments but you won't. That demon is trying to make you destroy yourself. *Spiritual suicide.*

There is a war going on between who you are being pulled by the world to be and who you are created to be. There is tremendous pull between the good and the bad until suddenly, the devil says, "kill yourself" and it sounds like the rational thing to do.

The thief does not come except to steal, and to kill, and to destroy.

(John 10:10a)

It does not matter how anointed you are, it does not matter how anointed the people around you are, the agenda is still the same and the devil is after you. This demon will not stop until He has gotten you. He will cause you to start blaming God for the choices that *you* made, and the stuff that *he* put you up to.

He will cause you to think that it is *God's* fault that you have no self control, no discipline. Then he will suggest that you turn your back on God. *This is your day to expose that devil for what he is. After you expose him, then you can expel him!*

DON'T GIVE YOURSELF AWAY

When I lost myself in high school, I gave away those things that were valuable to me. I did not *lose* those things; the devil did not *take* them. No, when I lost my identity, *I gave them away.* Not knowing who you are will make you not value what you have. The devil does not steal some things from you. Rather, your lack of identity causes you to make choices that in turn cause you to give it away.

I recently asked a group of young adults in our ministry a challenging question. Mind you, our ministry is comprised of individuals from the inner city and broken homes. Some are having their first encounter with Christ and church when they join us. So, I asked them, "Who was the person that you gave your first kiss to? "Who was the very first person you had sex with?

Do you realize you gave away something that you can never get back? You probably do not even know where that person is right now, yet you gave your first and best to them. I am willing to bet that you do not even know what their middle name was and you probably cannot remember their eye color either. So today anyone you claim you really love can only have 'used goods'. No one that you marry will get the best of you".

What a sobering thought. Ponder the question. Think it through. Do you remember who got your "firsts"?

THIS IS KILLING ME!

Then the spirit cried out, convulsed him greatly, and came out of him. And he became as one dead, so that many said, "He is dead."

(Mark 9:26)

Another characteristic of this spirit is it ***MAKES YOU THINK THAT GETTING DELIVERED WILL KILL YOU***. There are people who will not allow themselves to be delivered because that spirit tells them they cannot live without it.

They say such things as, "But I always drink to deal with my problems; this is what I always do when I get depressed". And so they are scared to let it go. This spirit will tell you that you cannot live unless you keep doing the things that are killing you.

For some, the fear of living free, prosperous or successful is so frightening until they willfully stay in bondage. That will not be your portion, in Jesus' Mighty Name!

GIVE HIM HIS WALKING PAPERS

Can you imagine all these characteristics of this one demon in this one boy? No wonder his father was desperate for Jesus? What about you - do you see yourself anywhere in this text?

You have to know this demon for what it is. And now that you know, if you do not give him his walking papers, if you keep doing what you have always done, then you are not only telling that demon, "I don't want you to go", you are telling him, "I *want* you to have control of my life."

It may sound hopeless. But the good news is,

...This kind can come out...

(Mark 9:29)

Whatever it is that is in you, it *can* come out. Your situation, the upheaval of your child, the chaos in your home is not impossible to be resolved. There is an answer. There is a solution. You can be free!

JUST BELIEVE

Then the disciples came to Jesus privately and said, "Why could we not cast it out?" [20] *So Jesus said to them, "Because of your unbelief..."*

(Matthew 17:19-20)

The first thing you must do in order to get *that* demon out is ***BELIEVE***. It will not come out if you do not believe you can be free. The first step to your deliverance is to acknowledge, "I believe I can be free". You must have a consistent foundation of faith.

The Scripture teaches us that if you touch and agree regarding anything here on earth, it will be done in heaven. You need to have someone in your life who wants to see you *get* free as badly as you desire to *be* free!

...By the mouth of two or three witnesses the matter shall be established.

(Deuteronomy 19:15b)

Again I say to you that if two of you agree on earth concerning anything that they ask, it will be done for them by My Father in heaven.

(Matthew 18:19)

That is why when I preach I may symbolically say, "Touch a neighbor and tell him..."

When you do not want to touch or agree, it is as if you are saying, "I don't believe there is any power in heaven or earth that can get me delivered." The spirit wants to keep you from speaking out because it knows that you hold the power of death and life in your tongue. (Proverbs 18:21). Until you speak, you will not set your deliverance in motion. If you want to 'see it' you have to 'say it'!

And they overcame him by the blood of the Lamb and by the word of their testimony.

(Revelation 12:11a)

CONSTANT COMMUNION

This kind can come out by nothing but prayer…

(Mark 9:29)

The second criterion for your deliverance is ***A CONSISTENT PRAYER LIFE***. That little seven-minute prayer you do, or the praying you do while you are taking a shower or waiting for the bus is not going to get that demon out of you. You need to have a consistent prayer *life*. You must have constant communion with the Father. There needs to be a specific time and place that you have covenanted with God that you will meet Him daily!

Personally, I am well aware that I need to talk with God every day, throughout the day, in addition to my daily devotion. If I do not talk to Him and listen to His response, soon other people's voices start getting in my ears.

If I am not careful, I will start listening to the crazy conversations they have, causing me to delve deeper into the rubbish I am trying to get rid of. You need to have a prayer life that is conducive to the situation which you are dealing with.

Whatever trials you are going through, you need to be able to speak to God about those situations. You cannot rely on your mother's prayer life or your father's prayer life; those demons will wreak havoc in you if you do not have your *own* prayer life.

And the evil spirit answered and said, "Jesus I know, and Paul I know; but who are you?"

(Acts 19:15)

DEPRIVE YOURSELF

This kind can come out by nothing but prayer and fasting.

(Mark 9:29)

Finally, ***YOU MUST BE COMMITTED TO CONSECRATING YOUR FLESH.*** It is funny how we all want to be delivered but none of us wants to deprive our flesh. It is amazing that, those who are struggling the hardest, absolutely will not fast. Once you start threatening your flesh, it will quickly get in line.

Tell your flesh, "no soda, no chewing gum, no candy, no newspaper, no television, no parties, and no clubs." If you want to be delivered, you must make your flesh weak until your spirit is willing. Make your flesh die until your spirit rises up. Crucify your flesh until your spirit says, "I've got the victory". Of course the flesh will "go through" all kinds of ailments, aches, sicknesses and the like.

All these things are merely the symptoms of "withdrawal" as the body is being cleansed of all the pollutants that we "feed" it on a daily basis. Yet, after a few days, what we felt we could not live without, we find ourselves asking, "Why was I doing that?" ***I decree that this season you are about to enter will be so glorious, it will make you forget what you used to think was your best! In, the Mighty Name of Jesus!***

PRAYER POINT

Father! Let my future shine so ***brightly*** *that it blinds me to my past! In Jesus' Mighty Name!*

SCRIPTURE REFERENCE

Proverbs 4:18

Chapter Seven

Careful - The Devil Knows Your Address

THE DEVIL IS REAL

One of the greatest devices of the enemy down through the years has been to try to beguile, bewitch and bamboozle the minds of Christians so that they will not take him seriously. Today, Hollywood has been so infiltrated with movies of the occult, spirits and ghosts that we discount and minimize movies dealing with the demonic by stating: "it's only a movie."

Consequently, we look at Satan's activity as something that has a beginning and an end that it starts with the introduction, like a movie, and ends with the running of the credits. What the devil is trying to do is lull you into taking both credit and blame for his works. He will present you with an idea, instigate it and then when it goes awry, he will seek to cause you to think it was *your* idea.

Then you will spend the majority of your life trying to correct something that you did not even start. You will try to engage in solving with your flesh what is not a physical problem, but a *spiritual* one.

WHAT'S ON THE AGENDA TODAY?

The reality is that *there is a devil.* There really *are* demons. There really *is* an adversary who has an agenda. He comes to steal, kill and destroy (John 10:10). The devil has an agenda and if you do not have a goal and an agenda, you are automatically open for him to give you one.

If you do not have a plan for what you are going to do after high school, he has a plan ready for you. If you do not have a plan for what you are going to do during or after college, there is a demonic plan set for you.

If you do not know what you are going to do after work tonight, there is a demonic agenda to give you something to do the moment you punch out. If you do not know what you are going to dream about, whatever you viewed on television or viewed on the web will infiltrate your subconscious, because the enemy does not sleep.

He is the enemy of God – "*He who keeps you will not slumber*" (Psalm 1221:3), but your adversary, the devil, who is destined to hell (Revelation 20:1-3), neither slumbers nor sleeps either.

THERE'S NOTHING TO DO!

You cannot tell yourself you are merely taking a break to find yourself before you start doing your next thing.

Because while you are taking your break, the devil will fill your time with things that were never your design. This is one of the enemy's greatest devices for this generation that he could not use before, because today people have so many options and opportunities that they wind up doing nothing at all. People are bored.

The previous generations did not have an X-box or a Play station or a Madden. For entertainment they would step on a couple of old soda cans, put them on their heels, and act like they had tap shoes on. They did not have clubs or movie houses that open twenty-four hours a day.

Instead, when the street lights went on at eight o'clock, Mom and Grandma would clap their hands and all the young people would run into the house while every store shut down. It is amazing that the more this generation has, the more bored they are! Unfortunately, the more bored they are, the more tempting the enemy's suggestion to use their technology for perversion becomes.

WRITE IT DOWN!

The old saying. "the idle mind is the devil's playground" still holds true. Whenever you do not have a plan, there will be a very strategic phone call, "What are you doing?" The next thing you know, you are on your way to some place that you would have never gone, had you had a plan.

That is why scripture teaches us,

Write the vision and make it plain…

(Habakkuk 2:2)

Make a plan. Write it down. What are you going to do?

FLYING BLIND

The enemy has blinded our eyes. But the Bible tells us if the truth of God is hidden; it is only hidden to those who are already perishing,

...whose minds the god of this age has blinded, who do not believe, lest the light of the gospel of the glory of Christ, who is the image of God, should shine on them.

(2 Corinthians 4:3-4)

The goal of the enemy is two-fold. It is to one, get you to the point where you are not even open to receive God. But secondly, it also is to get you to the point, where you have gotten so "religious", that you "know enough Bible", to discount what people tell you, but not enough to cause you to choose to live holy. Then, my friend, you are truly blinded. There are some people who cannot be reached with the Word because they have been in or around the church all their lives. So now they can go through the motions, and they think that because they go through the motions, they actually are delivered.

The devil knows your address! He knows what to present to you at certain times because he knows what will happen if you ever open your eyes or if you ever get a revelation of the knowledge of truth. So he surrounds you with people and you begin to gravitate to those who do not see how your deliverance can happen and will convince you that because *they* cannot see it, you cannot see it either.

In John, Chapter 6, verse 56, when Jesus said, "*...eat My flesh and drink My blood...*" some of them said, *"This is a hard saying, who can bear it?"* (v. 60) and because it was hard for *them* to do it, they assumed it was hard for everyone else as well.

Just because one individual decides not to live holy, does not mean that another individual cannot live holy. Just because you cannot finish school does not mean I cannot finish school.

Listen, do not allow another individual's failures (be it family, friends or spiritual leader) to be the measuring stick for your successes. *Do not let someone else's experience be your expectation!*

PROTECT ME PLEASE

This type of teaching is not popular because not only does it not feel good to the flesh, but it touches the emotions as well. The flesh will get to the point where it will shut down, cross its arms, and then the emotions will start saying, "This doesn't feel good. Why do you have to be so rough?" *The flesh and the emotions are trying to protect that demonic spirit.*

When there is a strong man in control on the inside, he will make you sacrifice your flesh and your emotions so that you do not expose him. He will force you to cut yourself, burn yourself, lay with anyone, smoke anything, and drink anything.

Why? So that you will protect, at all costs, that demonic spirit who has taken up residence in your life. As I stated in the previous chapter, the enemy comes to steal and to kill and to destroy. He does not want there to be any sign of you left. He will steal your joy, your peace, your self-worth, your femininity, and your masculinity.

He wants your hope, your future and your aspirations dead. He will kill your desires, your vision, your love for your family, your desire for a new job, your desire for a new home. His goal is to destroy the way you feel about other people, every car that you get, every home that you are in, every job that you get.

HE KNOWS WHERE YOU LIVE

As we found in the previous chapter, getting delivered from the enemy is not an issue.

Then the spirit cried out, convulsed him greatly, and **came out** *of him.*

(Mark 9:26a)

Even Jesus said,

> *This kind* **can come out**... (Mark 9:29).

The problem is that you must purpose to *stay* delivered. Why? Because *if he was ever there, that devil knows your address. He knows where you live*!

Likewise, there are certain people you have been with who know how to "push your buttons", buttons other people cannot even touch. You have not truly been delivered as long you continue to associate with some people, frequenting where you have always been.

You must be proactive in maintaining your deliverance. You have to say to yourself, "If I have to change my phone number, fine. If I change the lock and I do not have enough strength to keep the door closed when you come knocking, I will move. But at all cost, I must be free."

DON'T BE A FOOL

The fool has said in his heart, "There is no God."

(Psalm 14:1)

A fool is not just someone who is mentally challenged. *The real fool is the one who knows the truth but will not walk in it.* You may try to act as if you have no knowledge. However, you *know* better, but you choose not to *do* better.

So the devil has a field day with you because you have already shown by your actions that you do not want to walk in what you know. He relies on you knowing but not doing and that way he is able to constantly keep you in his grips.

Anything that has its hand on you can manipulate you. Your peers manipulate you. The desires of your flesh manipulate you. You no longer have any control; like a puppet on a string, whichever fingers the *puppet master* moves, you are forced to move right along with them. *You need to cut those strings with the sword of the Spirit and run in freedom!*

GIVE HIM AN EVICTION NOTICE

That spirit will leave, but it is not going to leave without a struggle. Nobody, even when they have not paid their rent, enjoys being evicted. So even people who have not paid their bills try to act as if they have a right to be there. Many are content to let that demon stay because of the public exposure that will occur when he is brought out into the light.

Many do their business behind closed doors as long as they can walk back out and still maintain their image and public persona, they are satisfied. That is an image issue. But when real deliverance comes, it not only opens the door, it takes the door off the hinges. That demon will make you feel like dying. But if you are more determined to be free than you are to complain about how you feel, you can make the demon run from you.

Therefore submit to God. Resist the devil and he will flee from you.

(James 4:7)

All you have to do is get closer to God.

TAKE A BATH!

When an unclean spirit goes out of a man, he goes through dry places, seeking rest, and finds none. [44]*Then he says, "I will return to my house from which I came." And when he comes, he finds it empty, swept, and put in order.* [45]*Then he goes and takes with him seven other spirits more wicked than himself, and they enter and dwell there; and the last state of that man is worse than the first. So shall it also be with this wicked generation.*

(Matthew 12:43-45)

An unclean spirit is not just something dirty, but it is also something that is contrary to the moral standard of God. Anything you are doing that is against God's holy Word is uncleanness. This is not just *any* unclean thing however, it is an *unclean spirit.* It is bad enough when you are dealing with dirt you *can* see, but what do you do when you are dealing with something you *cannot* see?

An unclean spirit works in an invisible arena and is not recognized until it reveals itself in your flesh. You do not even realize it is in you until your activities start showing it. There can be no works of uncleanness unless there is a spirit that is unclean inside you.

DID YOU TAKE THE PLEDGE?

If, after reading this book, and you know that the spirit of God is reaching for you, yet you remain unchanged or unchallenged, it is because you have "pledged your allegiance to the adversary, who is a perverter of all that is righteous, and to his kingdom, for the temporary time that it stands – one nation under Lucifer, always divisive, with no liberty and no justice at all."

If you have made such an agreement to stay as you are, there comes a point that God cannot deliver you against your will. When you have both opportunity and options, and you oppose an invitation to come out from what you are in, to walk into what He wants you to be, you leave no other recourse but for Him to leave you to the mindset of debased living! (Romans 1:24-32)

TO EVERY THING THERE IS A SEASON

We spend too much time working on symptoms. God declares, "You have been picking fruit. Now I want you to go down and get to the root of the tree." You may think that just because there is no more manifestation of fruit, the tree is dead. However, every tree looks dead in the winter, but they blossom back again in the spring and have their greatest produce in the summer.

If you were to look at life as being based on seasons of culture, then because you have not established what your time and season in God is going to be, you are now set up by the agenda of the times and seasons of society. You probably have a tendency to get serious about God (if at all) in the fall and winter. The year is ending, resolutions are made. Then by the time spring comes, you feel an *itch.* When summer comes, you are full blown into what you had said you no longer wanted to be doing.

It is an ongoing pattern; you take a break from God during spring and summer and then come back again in the winter time. However, this does not have to be your testimony. Our God does not *move* by seasons; seasons are *controlled* by Him! Daniel 2:21 states, "*...He changes the times and the seasons...*" ***I decree: This will be the beginning of a new season for you, in Jesus' Mighty Name.***

INSIDE AND OUT

In this passage regarding the unclean spirit, Jesus was speaking to people who were religious but not regenerated. They had gone through *reformation* but not *regeneration*. Being religious merely means that they did things by habit. They went to church by habit; they read the Word by habit. They did those things because they knew they needed to do them. Those habits made them *try* to reform.

Reformation means trying to do the right thing for the purpose of being seen as right. These people tried to do the right things, but for the purpose of their political agendas. However, religion and reformation are outside works. Regeneration is an inside work. Jesus forced them to face the truth. He told them in no uncertain terms that they had put *aside* certain things but had changed nothing on the *inside*.

If you are trapped in religion, you are still the same on the inside, you are just doing things differently on the outside. Some think that sounds like a good thing. "Well, at least I'm not doing those things anymore." Sure, but what has happened on the inside? Just because you do not *do* certain things does not mean that you *are not* those things.

Sometimes you simply have not had the opportunity. It is not enough to just stop *doing* certain things if there is not a change on the inside as well.

ARE YOU TALKING TO ME?

When an unclean spirit goes out of a man...

(Matthew 12:43)

…or a woman… I know that some of you, when you read "out of a *man,*" you immediately said, "Well this is not for me", because you are thinking that this is a gender specific passage of Scripture. This is a symptom of a very subtle spirit.

If individuals affected by this *religious spirit* are not directly referred to, not specifically named, they will not be able to see themselves in the description. If you talk about various perversions but do not name the particular one they are plagued with, they will say, "He was not talking to me". This passage makes reference to *mankind* and applies to all of us.

WATER-PROOF

When an unclean spirit goes out of a man, he goes through dry places, seeking rest, and finds none.

(Matthew 12:43)

This spirit is looking for a place where there is no "moisture", no *anointing.* He is looking for someone whose praise and devotion are dry, who has no real zeal or hunger for God. That spirit may have come out *of* you but he believes he can come back, because there is nothing fresh happening in your life. And whenever there is nothing fresh happening, then you gravitate to what you have always known.

Many never want to make it to the praise and worship session of a worship service, they claim they only need the Word. Sure, they come for the Word but the ground of their heart is hard because it has not been turned over by praise and worship. When the preacher comes, he sows the seed but it falls on hard ground, stony ground or the wayside, because they were too lazy to partake in some prayer, some praise, some worship.

So when the Word comes forth, they are thinking about what they will do when the service is over. There is a spirit that says, "If I can just get you to shut out what's going on, I can keep you dry. I can keep you unmoved and then I can keep you to myself".

RIVERS OF LIVING WATER

The remedy is, you must make it your business to live a life of praise and worship, so that you can truly get into the Word of God. But more importantly, you must do all that you can so that the Word of God can get into you. Worship moistens the fallow ground of your heart and prepares it for the "seed" of the Word to be sown.

He who believes in Me, as the Scripture has said, out of his heart will flow rivers of living water.

(John 7:38)

Some will never give birth to their dreams because their womb is dry. Some believers may have dreams but the dryness of their spiritual womb will make their delivery a horrible struggle. There are visions you are supposed to be bringing forth, but you cannot because your water broke too soon and that 'baby' did not have time to come out. Then as soon as your water broke, you wanted to push the vision back in, to enjoy feeling like you were "pregnant" even though it was past time to bring forth what was promised.

COME WITH ME

… he goes through dry places, seeking rest…

(Matthew 12:43)

Notice that the text does not say *a* dry place, but dry *places*. That spirit inside you will automatically gravitate to other people who are as dry as you are. That is why you will often find yourself attracted to people who are nothing like the ones you thought you would be with. It was not their *appearance* that you gravitated to, it was their spirit. *Like spirits are attracted to one another.*

Now, I know that some will say, "I don't believe in all that spirit stuff". But here is a saying that carries that very same concept and has found its way into mainstream thinking and communication: "birds of a feather flock together".

YOU'RE ALL MINE

This spirit believes that he has both ownership of and access to you whenever he wants; he thinks that you are his property. He will not even allow you to think for yourself, he will lead you to believe you cannot make a good decision. This spirit will even make you ask other people whether you can do what God told you to do. It will make you so insecure that you will live for the enablement of other people.

This is a spirit who tells you that you are too ugly, too dark, too light, too skinny, too fat, too *something*, because it wants to keep control of you. As long as it can keep you from knowing who you are in God, then you are open to whatever other spirits it sends in your direction. Every spirit thinks it owns you; however the Bible says you have the Holy Ghost as a guarantee (II Corinthians 5:5). The proof that you are not controlled by that spirit is that even when you have gone astray, something inside of you says, "I still have to find my way back to God".

As long as you can find a praise or prayer, you can find a way to call on God. You may have to tell someone, "Pull the car over.

I'd rather walk back than to ride in a car that's got all these bad spirits inside of it", but you will have to do whatever it takes to get back in relationship with God.

Some remain in a "stuck" state because of the fear of being by themselves or the threat of the struggle they perceive that it will take to be free. But you must let that "terrorist" spirit know that, "I would rather be by myself and free than to remain in this state of bondage."

OH, THAT IRRESISTIBLE SPIRIT

I will return to my house from which I came.

(Matthew 12:44a)

This spirit is so controlling, he thinks you cannot resist him. He thinks that he can walk in and out of your life any time he wants to. Similarly, there are some people who have been put out of your life, yet they think they can come back anytime. And as soon as you see a message from them, you get excited or scared - excited because you wonder what they are feeling; scared because you do not think you have the ability to tell them, "Stay away from me".

There is something inside of you that still does not know that you have been delivered, and when you do not know that you are delivered, you will continue to gravitate to the people that you asked God to take away from you, and take you away from! Part of the problem is that you have run the devil out but you have not invited anyone new in. Where there is no presence of the Holy Ghost, there *is* an invitation to the unholy Ghost.

IT'S DECISION TIME

There is no neutral territory. You cannot say, "Well I'm just sort of in the middle."

No you are wholly in the enemy's camp. Because there is no middle ground.

Jesus declares:

He who is not with Me is against Me...

(Matthew 12:30)

End of discussion.

If you have not given your life to the Lord, you have given your life to the devil.

TAKE DOWN THE VACANCY SIGN

So it is not enough to get out of your mess if you do not fill that void with something (someone, Jesus) positive! It is not enough to stop going to the club if you do not start going to church more often. You cannot just stay in your house and say, "I don't go out".

If you do not go someplace at the times you used to attend the places that were negative, you have essentially left a vacancy sign on your body, soul and spirit, which means that the demons can come in. Even though you are not where they were, they know your address. You need to go somewhere new and let something better get inside of you. Many believers have missed this, which is why they are still struggling.

DON'T SWEEP IT UNDER THE RUG

And when he comes, he finds it empty, swept, and put in order.

(Matthew 12:44b)

The fact that he finds it swept means there has been no activity. My wife has a company come in and clean our home. I can tell whenever they have vacuumed because there are marks and grooves on the carpet and there are no footprints. The carpet is in nice, vacuumed rows. I can also tell if anyone has been in one of the rooms after the cleaning, because their feet disrupt the well-vacuumed rows.

I can tell if there has been activity in that room. Once you get the activity of unclean spirits out and clean up where they were, if no new positive activity is introduced, then that spirit will assume that there is not anything happening in your life. The problem with so many individuals is that they get delivered but they do not get active in the things of God. The purpose of being *free from* the snare of the enemy is so that one can be *free for* the work of the kingdom.

In the spring of the year when kings usually go out to war, David was supposed to be out fighting with the energy he had saved up from the winter. Instead, he sent out his assistants to fight on his behalf.

In his restless, energetic state, he walked up on the porch, saw a naked woman taking a bath, took her for himself and then got her pregnant. Then his only option seemed to be to have her husband killed. God's Word found him, confronted him and convicted him.

This one act set forth a series of destructive patterns in his family and administration (2 Samuel 11-17). If you have the energy to do something worthwhile for God but you are not using that energy, you will end up using that energy for the ungodly acts of the devil.

By so doing we then set in motion a plethora of problems and plagues that can wreak havoc in, not only our lives, but like David, in our children and the generations to come.

EVERYTHING IN ITS PLACE

... he finds it empty, swept, and ***put in order***.

(Matthew 12:44b)

The devil returns and finds everything in order: a place for everything and everything in its place. Why is that significant? Because this spirit is more concerned about image than content. Image is the root word of imagination. Some have lost their identity because they have been engaged in creating an image.

You are more concerned about fulfilling someone else's imagination than having your own identity. *Appearance*, "having a form of godliness" (2 Timothy 2:5) is more important to some than having the *power* to be all that they are created to be.

EASY ACCESS

Then he goes and takes with him seven other spirits more wicked than himself...

(Matthew 12:45a)

Apparently that demon has influence over other demons, even those that are stronger than he.

He goes out and gets seven more demons, more wicked than he is. Once you have allowed that *one* spirit to know your address; how you think or feel, your times of struggle, your patterns and proclivities, he introduced you to demons who had not even known you existed. *The devil does not know everything.*

In the Book of Job when the sons of God came together, God said to Satan, "Have you considered my servant, Job?" The devil did not even know who Job was (Job 1:6-12). *There are some spirits you have been introduced to, simply because of the original spirit you attracted.* When a demonic spirit finds something easy and good, he passes it on to every other demonic spirit who is looking for easy access.

EXCEEDINGLY WICKED

The spirit goes out, gets seven additional demons more wicked than himself and influences them to enter you. And now you spend your life fighting the seven new spirits because they are hiding the one who invited them.

You may think you know what your problem is. But your problem is not what you think it is. What you are seeing is just one of the demons.

Your real problem is not the pornography, not the alcohol, not the crack, not the clubs; it is not even the anger, the promiscuity, the insatiable appetite or the money – those are just the *symptoms.*

There is another deeper stronghold. Your real problem is your insecurity, distrust, low self-worth and the like. And those things are what you do to hide that insecurity.

SOWING INTO GOOD GROUND

God's word teaches us that, when the sower went out to sow the seed, there were four types of ground.

Only one type of soil was able to receive the seed and bring it to fruition (Matthew 13). Unfortunately, based on that biblical ratio, that means that only one in four readers of this book are going to understand and take advantage of this teaching.

Dear Reader, do not miss this opportunity!

Seek the LORD while He may be found, Call upon Him while He is near.

(Isaiah 55:6)

PRAYER POINT

Father! Rid me of everything that is not like You, and build Your home in me. My body…Your temple! In Jesus' Mighty Name.

SCRIPTURE REFERENCE:

Revelation 3:20

Chapter Eight

The Tactics of War

GEARED UP FOR BATTLE

For though we walk in the flesh, we do not war according to the flesh.
4For the weapons of our warfare are not carnal but mighty in God for
pulling down strongholds, 5casting down arguments and every high thing
that exalts itself against the knowledge of God, bringing every thought
into captivity to the obedience of Christ, 6and being ready to punish all
disobedience when your obedience is fulfilled.

(2 Corinthians 10:3-6)

Having the right weaponry is equally as important as knowing the devil that you are up against. It is one thing to know what kind of devil you are dealing with, but if you do not have or know how to use the proper tools, the necessary weaponry, to defeat that demon, then you might as well not have anything.

Without the right weapons and proper knowledge, you are still going to fail when it comes to dealing with the devil.

PROVEN TACTICS

The Scripture makes it clear that Satan comes only for the purpose of stealing, killing and destroying, and that he continues to use the same devices he has employed since creation. So the danger is not that he is so intelligent, or that he has such a wide variety of weaponry, or that he disguises the fact that he is out to destroy you; everything he is and does is right there on the table.

The real danger lies in our ability to see these strategies for what they are. *Satan does not need to change his methods, until you show him that his tactics do not work.* The enemy uses three specific devices in order to destroy us: "The lust of the flesh, the lust of the eyes and the pride of life" (1 John 2:16).

THE ORIGINAL SIN

So when the woman saw that ***the tree was good for food,*** *that* ***it was pleasant to the eyes,*** *and* ***a tree desirable to make one wise,*** *she took of its fruit and ate.*

(Genesis 3:6)

Even at Creation, Satan used these same three tactics on Eve:

Lust of the flesh:

the tree was good for food

Lust of the eyes:

it was pleasant to the eyes

Pride of life:

and a tree desirable to make one wise

THE TEMPTATION OF CHRIST

These tactics worked so well with the first man, Adam, in the Garden of Eden, when the second Adam, the Lord Jesus Christ, arrived on the scene, Satan came at Him with the exact same strategies:

Lust of the flesh:

And the devil said to Him, "If You are the Son of God, command this stone to become bread."

(Luke 4:3)

Lust of the eyes:

Then the devil, taking Him up on a high mountain, showed Him all the kingdoms of the world in a moment of time. [6]And the devil said to Him, "All this authority I will give You, and their glory; for this has been delivered to me, and I give it to whomever I wish".

(Luke 4:5-6)

Pride of life:

Then he brought Him to Jerusalem, set Him on the pinnacle of the temple, and said to Him, "If You are the Son of God, throw Yourself down from here. [10]For it is written: 'He shall give His angels charge over you, To keep you,' [11]and, 'In their hands they shall bear you up, Lest you dash your foot against a stone.'"

(Luke 4:9-11)

AH, THE INNOCENCE OF YOUTH

No matter what the age and stage of your life, the enemy does not change his approach. Both Eve and Jesus were in the virginity, the purity, the innocence of their walk with God. Eve, though she was a grown woman, was in the virginity of her walk with God because she had not spoken to any other god than God the Father.

Jesus was in the innocence, the virginity, the purity of His walk with God as well, although He declared at age twelve, "I must be about My Father's business" (Luke 2:49). He was just about to start His earthly ministry.

So in the infancy of their walks with God, the enemy sought to seduce them. He tried to intoxicate them with subtle words that were exactly what they were susceptible to at that time. He sought to take their virginity, their purity; to seduce them while they were in their innocence and to take something they could never regain.

HE'S JUST A SMOOTH TALKER

This is always Satan's goal, to steal the virginity of your walk; whether it is the virginity of your sex life, or your trust, or your faith. He comes with smooth words saying what you want to hear in *that* stage of your life. He seduces you by telling you that what he is offering you will make you feel good, look a certain way or add something to your stature.

The enemy wants to steal all of your *firsts*; your first kiss, your first sexual experience. He wants to take your first pure thought and then pervert it. He will bring someone in to betray your first area of trust to make you think you can never trust anyone. And sadly, anywhere the enemy is able to pervert seems irreparable.

The lust of the flesh, the lust of the eye and the pride of life; every time anyone has lost their virginity in any area, it was a result of one of these strategies.

BAMBOOZLED!

As a result, it seems that no one is thinking about purity, holiness, or keeping what God has given you for yourself. Instead, one tries to justify their actions by thinking that because they may have lost it, God must never have intended for you to keep it in the first place. Listen, you have been seduced into thinking that since everyone thinks and acts this way, it must be the norm. But you have been bamboozled!

The enemy has twisted your thinking to such an extent that you truly believe you cannot be what God intended you to be.

I'LL STRAIGHTEN YOU OUT

For every plan that God has for your life, the devil has an agenda, and he does not disguise what his agenda is: steal, kill and destroy. Thankfully, however, it does not matter how badly the enemy has twisted you with his entangling lies. God is perfectly capable of straightening your mind if you will allow Him. You cannot go back to being a virgin physically, but He will wash everything away and let you start all over again.

"Come now, and let us reason together," Says the LORD, "Though your sins are like scarlet, They shall be as white as snow; Though they are red like crimson, They shall be as wool."

(Isaiah 1:18)

CAN YOU STOP ME?

Years ago, a Washington football team that I really enjoy had a couple of outstanding running backs, Larry Brown and John Riggins. These running backs were so consistently good that Coach Allen and Coach Gibbs could give the ball to either of them and everyone knew exactly what was going to happen. These were that particular teams favorite plays.

The other team just had to decide whether they could stop them or not. They knew exactly what plays the team was going to run, yet they usually could not stop it anyhow.

Similarly the enemy says:

> Even if you know what I am going to do, I want to know, can you stop it? I'll tell you what my plan is. I'll tell you how I'm going to attack. I'll even let you see

it in your family line through generational curses. All I want to know is are you strong enough to be different? If I show you I'm making everyone else have sex, are you strong enough to keep yourself a virgin? Even if I'm showing you that I'm making everyone pregnant, are you strong enough to keep yourself pure? I'm letting you see everybody else get drunk. Are you courageous enough to not take a drink? I'm going to run these same plays again and again until you stop me. You've seen it in your aunts and uncles. There is a pattern with all men and women in your family. No one has graduated. No one has owned their own home. No one has stayed married, overcome breast cancer, etc. Do you dare to break the family curse?

I'M HIGHLY OFFENDED!

The good news is *that there is a defense for every offensive attack of the devil.* And yes, he is *offensive.* You ought to be offended that he has messed up your life like this!

You ought to be offended that he has made you think you do not have a future.

You ought to be offended that you have seen the enemy mess with your grandmother and then your mother and now you see yourself heading down that same path.

You ought to be offended that your father was not in your life and now you are making kids but will not stay in their lives either.

You have a right to be offended!

THE SAME TIRED, OLD THING

One can receive as much counsel as they want to, be put in twelve steps, seventeen steps, 100 ways of deliverance, but they will not change until *they* get tired.

I can be tired of what you do, but until *you* get tired, you are going to keep on doing the same thing over and over again. I can love, I can weep, I can do anything I want but you will keep acting the same way until you get tired. It becomes a pattern, you do what you do, you say, "Man, I'm tired of doing this, I'm tired of living like this," but you do not stop. This is what the enemy relies on, that you are ignorant to his tired old play.

AS LONG AS NO ONE GETS HURT

One of the greatest lies the enemy has gotten individuals to confess is this: "Well, I'm not hurting anybody, only myself." But do you know how many people are tied into you? Do you know how many people are watching you? How many brothers or sisters heard what you said you were standing for and then watched you when you fell? A statement like that is born from the 'soil' of selfishness. It reeks with the stench of inconsideration, with no regard for anyone's well being except your own!

How many people are looking at you thinking you will be the one to show them how to get out of their situation? Some wise sage declared, "No man is an island." We do not live to ourselves. It is a part of the character of the devil to cause an individual to selfishly think that their life does not affect anyone else. We are all a part of the "human" family, even if we are not a part of the body of Christ!

A PAWN IN THE HANDS OF THE ENEMY

Lest Satan should take advantage of us; for we are not ignorant of his devices.

(2 Corinthians 2:11)

The aforementioned passage speaks a powerful truth; satan's advantage is *birthed* in our ignorance. He does not have an advantage if you are not ignorant of his devices. But the moment you do not know his devices, you then become a pawn in his hands That is why it is so dangerous if you do not have a prayer life or read the Word of God or study to show yourself,

...approved to God, a worker who does not need to be ashamed, rightly dividing the word of truth.

(2 Timothy 2:15)

Do you think that it is mere coincidence that you just 'happen' to get sleepy when it comes to reading the Word of God? But it is not as simple as that. The enemy knows that if he can get you to play into your flesh being tired, you will remain ignorant concerning his devices.

AROUND AND AROUND

So Paul states that Satan's victory is birthed in the womb of our pride and our arrogant stupidity. The enemy is well aware that you have some arrogant, self righteous, "you-can't-tell-me –nothing" issues, and he uses that to his advantage.

It is not that he makes you bored in church, it is just that he knows that if he can cause you to think that church is not exciting, you will not come. And if you will not come, then you will have no spiritual intelligence. If you have no intelligence, you will be ignorant - not to the world, but to his devices.

It is a *demonic domino syndrome.* Failure or falling in one area starts the downward motion of other things in another area.

Consequently, when you *try* to come to church, to you it really *is* boring, because you have equated your enthusiasm or excitement to the things of the world, and the church is not acting like the world. Many people want to come in church and continue to act like they do in the world. They want to look like the world, dress like the world, talk like the world.

However, there is a spirit attached to the mindset cultivated in the environment that you came from. Since your mind has not been changed, you are coming into church but remaining the same way in your thinking and reasoning. That is why the Apostle Paul declares:

And do not be conformed to this world, but be transformed by the renewing of your mind, that you may prove what is that good and acceptable and perfect will of God.

(Romans 12:2)

Meanwhile, God is trying to penetrate your carnality. "Carnal" means "flesh," referring to "meat." Esau gave up his birthright for a bowl of beans to appease his flesh. It was his flesh with beans that made him give up his birthright. Likewise, you can choose to give up your future for something that satisfies your flesh, but does not promise you any lasting sustenance.

ALWAYS BE PREPARED

I repeat, Satan's advantage is birthed in the womb of ignorance. So many cannot even quote a Scripture and will not carry a Bible, even to church. Strange, though, that no one goes to the functions that the world has to offer without being prepared. You do not go to work at Microsoft if you have not been prepared on Microsoft.

You prepare yourself for where you are going. Why is it that one thinks that church is a place you can come without being prepared? Or that this Christian life can be "lived" victoriously without studying?

CONSTRUCTED FOR A SPECIFIC PURPOSE

...for we are not ignorant of his devices.

(2 Corinthians 2:11)

The word *device* according to *Webster's Second New Riverside Dictionary* is "something constructed for a specific purpose."

In other words, the enemy designs a device specifically for you from one of those three areas; the lust of the flesh, the lust of the eye and the pride of life. If you are lonely, he does not bring you a companion that you do not want. Listen, a temptation is not a temptation if it is not something that appeals to you! For example, Satan cannot tempt an individual with what he or she does not have an attraction to or an affinity for.

However, if by observing one's times, seasons and patterns he notes what you have a propensity or proclivity for, then he can bring it in different colors, shapes, and sizes, and one will be vulnerable to that. There even comes a time when you are so vulnerable to the enemy's devices that you will throw off your usual specifications and will take whatever is available, even though it does not meet your standard.

If you do not have *knowledge* of the enemy and *understanding* of yourself, there are times when you will be susceptible to just about anything. For example, one may want crack (cocaine) if crack is their thing, but if they cannot get crack, they will eventually take a joint (marijuana).

Because the enemy is hitting them so hard in the area of their weakness, they are vulnerable to just about anything he brings.

Many of you say you are looking for a quality man who favors some movie star idol, or a beautiful woman that meets a certain criteria. But if that is the case, why are you with someone that does not meet that standard? Why have you settled? The reason is because you do not know who you are in God. Loneliness sets in, or time is running out; so the enemy has every opportunity to tempt you where you are with what is not your choice, but a sufficient substitute…for the time. ***Listen, please, do not allow a temporary need to cause you to make a permanent choice***!

The devil does not have to be *selective*; he just has to be *seductive*. And that is why *your* sin makes you feel so guilty, because not only did you transgress, but you lowered your standards to get there.

DON'T FORFEIT!

The enemy's device is something constructed for a specific *purpose*, but the Bible says that we are called according to *God's purpose (Romans 8:28)*. So the enemy devises his purpose based on where he senses you are going, in order to make you abort your true purpose. His goal is to devise a plan that will make you forfeit God's plan for you (Jeremiah 29:11).

The closer you get to your destiny, the more intense the strategy becomes. When you are off track and not headed towards your destiny, he can give you anything and you will be drawn in. But the closer you get to your true purpose, the more selective he has to be, because the more knowledgeable and careful *you* will be.

So the enemy saves his best devices for when you are just about to step in to your destiny. For someone holding this book, the attacks that you are experiencing are a direct result of you being on the threshold of your destiny. *Don't lose you focus!*

IT'S IN YOUR BLOOD

In Jesus' early ministry, His mother and His brothers came seeking Him (Luke 8:19-21). He kept on ministering, however, saying, "Who's my mother? Who's my brother? Those who will do the will of My Father." He then started pouring into His disciples. One betrayed Him, one denied Him and the rest forsook Him.

Once Jesus changed His allegiance from His blood relatives to those who would be His first disciples then called "friends", then the devil used them too. The enemy's strategy is to attempt to break you by getting to your family, your own blood your support system.

If that doesn't work, he moves on to the next level. Oftentimes when our family is our whole foundation, the devil will institute a breakup. Why? Even he knows that when a house is divided, there can be no stability (Matthew 12:25).

So we go and pour ourselves into people that are *like* family, and the pattern continues. The devil causes them to not only do that which makes you feel abandoned or rejected, but to ultimately bring about distrust by association. Please understand, the same thing happening to an individual from personal yet different sources, can cause them to develop the mantra that everyone is the same and God doesn't care. Hence, causing a mistrust of God and an abortion of purpose.

IT'S A PERSONAL MATTER

When those who were like family broke His heart, Jesus said, "That's ok My meat is to do the will of the Father," (John 4:24). So He goes to the cross of Calvary, on the verge of His true destiny, and God, His Father, turns His back on Him too. Why? For the purpose of fulfilling prophecy and destiny. *I repeat, the closer you get to your destiny, the more personal the attacks become and the more painful the strategy of the adversary.*

The closer you get to where you are going, the more it will take to break your power. Personally, I know I must be close to where God is taking me, because the enemy is pulling out all the stops. He is putting every relationship, from both past and present, on display, and making me look at my future. He wants to know if I merely want to be free from hurt or do I want to *hurdle* what is in front of me. Many have such a low threshold for pain until they fail to realize that sometimes pain is a necessary process to progress!

And I have decided that even though I am hurting, I will hurdle; I'll leap over them all. I believe that for someone holding this book now, this last segment has made sense of what has been going on in your life lately. May the Almighty God cause you to "run through troops" and "leap over walls" in Jesus' Mighty Name.

IT IS KNOWLEDGE THAT YOU ARE LACKING

My people are destroyed for lack of knowledge. Because you have rejected knowledge, I also will reject you from being priest for Me; Because you have forgotten the law of your God, I also will forget your children.

(Hosea 4:6)

Notice He is not only speaking of a lack of knowledge but of *rejected* knowledge. We always stop after "*My people are destroyed for the lack of knowledge.*" But there is more to it than that. God says that because you have rejected knowledge, He rejected you from being His priest.

In other words, there were some promotions you were supposed to get, but because you have rejected the knowledge of God, you not only did not get the promotion, you got fired. And now you cannot find a job!

LOOKING TO THE FUTURE

The issue is not that you did not *know* what was right, but that you are living like you never learned it. So not only are you prevented from being priest for Him, but because you have forgotten the law of your God, He is likewise going to forget, not only you, but your *children*. This speaks, not only of your heirs, but also your future, your lineage, your posterity, your hopes and your dreams.

So because you have rejected knowledge and refuse to retain God's laws in your life, not only will you miss those promotions, but you forfeit your future and your children's future. Your descendants will not have access to the opportunities they might have had, had you lived as *you* should.

David's hearts desire was to build the temple of God. But instead, because he was a man of war and had blood on his hands, God told him he was still to compile all the material for the temple, but that his son would be the one to build it. David lost out but the honor remained with his family because his heart was after the Lord's heart.

THE NEXT GENERATION

When you sin, it affects your family in a negative way. However, if you seek to please God, it sets them up in a positive way. Maybe I didn't cross every "T" and dot every "I" in my life, but when I was confronted with my transgressions, I pulled myself together, so that my children now have a positive destiny.

I may not be the one to build it, but if my children are standing in the name of the Lord Jesus Christ, representing the household of Sturdivant, even though I may be off the scene, I will still be able to hear the praises, "The Sturdivant's are doing a great thing."

The society we live in tells us we are not to consider anyone but ourselves. They call it "dog eat dog" and "every man for himself." But you must remember, there is another generation coming out of you some day. You may be too young to plan a family right now, but you are not too young to begin setting up their spiritual inheritance.

You may say, "I'm too old to have children" or "I've done so much wrong, to avoid the repercussions, I won't have any children."

Yet, there are still cousins, nieces, nephews, neighbors, coworkers, etc who are watching and gleaning from what you say and do, even if you are not aware of it. All of us influence someone either positively or negatively.

Remember this, *you can choose your choices, but you cannot choose your repercussions!* You cannot know how the choices you are making are going to affect you or future generations. Therefore choose wisely.

I call heaven and earth as witnesses today against you, that I have set before you life and death, blessing and cursing; therefore choose life, that both you and your descendants may live.

(Deuteronomy 30:19)

Choose life so that you and your children and your children's children can live. Your choices affect eternity.

PRAYER POINT

Father! Now that I know the enemy's tactics, help me to be proactive instead of reactive in my fight against him. In Jesus' Mighty Name, Amen!

SCRIPTURE REFERENCE

2 Timothy 2:4

Chapter Nine

Defeating Your Demons

THE WINNING STRATEGY

For though we walk in the flesh, we do not war according to the flesh. [4]*For the weapons of our warfare are not carnal but mighty in God for pulling down strongholds,* [5]*casting down arguments and every high thing that exalts itself against the knowledge of God, bringing every thought into captivity to the obedience of Christ,* [6]*and being ready to punish all disobedience when your obedience is fulfilled.*

(2 Corinthians 10:3-6)

This passage gives us a tactic to combat the devil's strategy. Once you are no longer ignorant of his devices, you need to know how to battle them. You cannot know *what* to do when the enemy attacks you, if you have not *planned* for it ahead of time.

PREPARATION IS THE KEY

When my children (they are grown now) were younger, as we were sitting together at home, I would tell them, "Listen, I want to tell you what things to look out for when you face certain challenges, so that when you get into that situation, you'll already know what to do. Once you are in that atmosphere, you will not be able to *think* clearly."

This is where many people, young and old, make mistakes; because they have the wrong idea that they will know what to do when the situation arises. The world has coined a phrase that states, "I will cross that bridge when I get to it."

This, however, is not true. If you wait until you are forced to make a choice, you will burn the bridge before you even think of crossing it. You cannot wait until you get in the situation, when your flesh is panting and you are in the heat of the moment, because your desire will not allow you to say, "Oh, I need to get out of here." At that point, your flesh will not allow your mind to think. Thinking does not work.

The lust of the flesh, the lust of the eyes, and the pride of life - these are the only three ruses the adversary has to trip us up.

THOSE CREATIVE JUICES ARE FLOWING!

With the enemy's seduction comes creativity, so you must have a plan to combat it. Unless you are determined *not* to cuss before the frustrating moment, you will not only cuss but create a new rude phrase. If you desire a certain type of individual but your seduction has been twisted, you will suddenly begin to desire every age, shape, size, color and ethnicity, and then you will want them all at once. Addictions and habits just like the demonic *cannot* and *will not* be compartmentalized. They are all territorial!

Next, you will decide that you need a drink before you hook up with your lover, then you'll want to do a line of cocaine, and it goes on and on, deeper and deeper. Once the enemy has twisted your thoughts, he will make sure to entice you to combine your sins, so that you continually desire to add sin to other sin, trying to equal that first experience.

When you have lost your virginity in virtually every area, you start opening up to new, less mainstream areas, such as homosexuality and pedophilia. It is not by accident that you think about trying other things. Your perversion, your twisted way of thinking, uses up everything that was common so that all that is left are the uncommon things (Romans 1:25-28).

NOTHING NEW UNDER THE SUN

You need a strategy because the *enemy* has a plan, one that has been working from Genesis all the way to today. He relies on fool hearted you and I to think we are safe simply because we look at those who have gone before and say, "Well that isn't going to happen to me." But unless we have a plan, we will have the same end.

Many people think they can come up with a device for trying to beat the devil. However, we each have only about seventy-five, maybe eighty years to accomplish this, while he has had centuries of experience, from the beginning of time until now. His strategies have already been proven to work.

Rather than waste your limited amount of time, you need to just go ahead and acknowledge that you are not smart enough to defeat the devil your own way.

FIGHT ON YOUR OWN TURF

When you use the right strategy, you *can* defeat the devil. You can get him out of your house and keep him from coming back.

For though we walk in the flesh, we do not war according to the flesh.

(2 Corinthians 10:3)

It is important to remember that you may be on the devil's *turf* but you cannot fight on his *terms*. Yes, the earth is the Lord's but the Lord does not have all the influence here. Now before you close the book, hear me out. There are two major forces pulling on this world.

God is everywhere but the influence of the devil is too, although he is not omnipresent. Yet, he has so many demons who have enlisted so many individuals until it "feels" like he's everywhere.

If you believe that the devil has no influence, you believe a lie. Satan's influence is obvious in the ungodly laws being made, the babies being aborted, the same sex marriages being established. Babies are being killed; four-year old children are being left out on the beltway. People simply walk away from their kids and act like they never had any. You may be on the devil's turf but you cannot fight on his terms.

Mad as HELL!

Therefore rejoice, O heavens, and you who dwell in them! Woe to the inhabitants of the earth and the sea! For the devil has come down to you, having great wrath, because he knows that he has a short time.

(Revelation 12:12)

Heaven rejoiced when the devil was kicked out. But woe to the earth, because now the devil is here, and he *is* mad as hell that he "got the boot." He is well aware and very angry at the fact that he only has a short time left in which to influence us.

But what really gets him the most is that you have access to go where he can no longer go. Where is that? Into the presence of the Lord! So now, his whole purpose is to keep you from getting to where he once used to be!

But even if our gospel is veiled, it is veiled to those who are perishing, [4]whose minds the god of this age has blinded, who do not believe, lest the light of the gospel of the glory of Christ, who is the image of God, should shine on them.

(2 Corinthians 4:3-4)

THE SON OF MORNING

In heaven, Lucifer was in charge of the praise team. He was called the "Son of the Morning." According to Ezekiel and Isaiah, his very body composed music, so that every instrument, every note, every piece of music got its orientation from Lucifer. Whenever he lifted his hand to conduct, the music came through him. Lucifer stood in front of the very throne of God, so when God spoke a word, it went through Lucifer, as praise, to get to its destiny.

And whenever earth responded to God, it came through Lucifer, as praise, to get back to Him. That is why when you want anything from God; you begin your request with praise (Psalm 100:4). The fact that you now have the ability to do what the devil can no longer do is very upsetting to him. You can praise while he cannot.

So he gets his identity back through you. When you come into the presence of God, you *are* praise, and you are carrying out the devil's former agenda. Because when you become praise, you are a replacement worship leader in the presence of God, and every time you do that, you remind the devil, "I got your job."

Now *his* job is to stop you from doing his former assignment. So that is why when you discover you have been fired, you praise anyhow.

When you do not get the loan you need, you praise anyhow. When the doctor tells you "You have a sickness," you praise anyhow. You are doing Lucifer's former job, and you are reminding him that God rules your situation from the *seat* you created with praise!

But You are holy, Enthroned in the praises of Israel.

(Psalm 22:3)

NOT ACCORDING TO FLESH

For though we walk in the flesh, we do not war according to the flesh.

(2 Corinthians 10:3)

I may be on the devil's turf but I will not fight on his terms, because my flesh cannot stand against his weapons. If I am not careful, he will use my flesh to get victory over me. Listen, it *is* possible for my own body to be my worst enemy in this Christian walk. That is why I must at all cost; give control of my flesh to the Lord! (Romans 7:18-25) So I cannot fight him on his terms.

According to Ephesians 6:12;

For we do not wrestle against flesh and blood, but against principalities, against powers, against the rulers of the darkness of this age, against spiritual hosts of wickedness in the heavenly places.

(Ephesians 6:12)

We are embattled in spiritual warfare and

No one engaged in warfare entangles himself with the affairs of this life, that he may please him who enlisted him as a soldier.

(2 Timothy 2:4)

True soldiers do not allow what is happening around them to make them go AWOL or run every time there is gun fire. Also, *true soldiers do not shoot fellow soldiers.*

GET BY WITH A LITTLE HELP FROM A FRIEND

We are often so busy assassinating the character and integrity of our brothers and sisters, that we do not see the forest for the trees. It is the enemy who goads us into turning on one another; so that we do not even understand that they are the very people who are going to help us defeat him.

The enemy always tries to infiltrate and ruin your closest relationships, because the closest relationships are the ones that put up with you, no matter what. When you finally kill the closest relationships, your more distant relationships are watching and do not want to come close. Why? They concur, "If you'll do that to them, there is no telling what you will do to me." So then, when you really need someone, you do not have anyone.

PUT ON THE WHOLE ARMOR

For the weapons of our warfare are not carnal but mighty in God for pulling down strongholds.

(2 Corinthians 10:4)

You must use what has been proven to not only *cover* you but *conquer* him. In other words, God's military armor is the only proven attire that can conquer our enemy.

His Word Commands:

Therefore take up the whole armor of God, that you may be able to withstand in the evil day, and having done all, to stand. (Ephesians 6:13)

God has prepared armor based on the character of who *He* is and when you arm yourself with His attire, you are then able to do to the devil what God did.

Putting on God's armor gives you the ability to conquer what God conquers (Philippians 4:13). When you put God's armor on you, you get *God-type results*, not just *good results.*

DAVID AND GOLIATH

King Saul was scared of Goliath. He had garments that he had worn in other victories, but he was too afraid to battle the Philistine champion himself.

So he tried to put his armor on David, saying, "If you're going to go after Goliath, put on the armor that I've had victories in and then you can have the victories I've had."

Have you ever wondered - why didn't Saul put on his own armor and compete against Goliath himself? In his heart, he knew this victory hinged not on the armor, but in a relationship, an anointing that he no longer had. David, on the other hand, knew his relationship was right.

He knew that the same God who had helped him kill the bear and the lion would give him this victory. David had the heart but no armor; Saul had the armor but no heart. But in the end, David knew that what he had was all he needed. And he went against Goliath with what God had given him and made it work for him.

GUARD YOUR LOINS WITH TRUTH

The Scripture Teaches That We Must:

Stand therefore, having ***girded your waist with truth****, having put on the breastplate of righteousness.* (Ephesians 6:14)

"Loins" speaks to your abdominal area, the foundation which holds the upper part and lower part of your body together. Your loins, or waist, are right around your navel - beneath your nipples and above your sexual organs.

If you have truth in your foundation, your core, you will know the truth about your sexual orientation and the truth about how you feel in your heart. But if you do not have the truth there, then your heart will tell your loins to do something that they are not designed by God to do.

YOU'RE OUT OF YOUR MIND!

...casting down arguments and every high thing that exalts itself against the knowledge of God, bringing every thought into captivity to the obedience of Christ, [6]and being ready to punish all disobedience when your obedience is fulfilled.

(2 Corinthians 10:5-6)

Many mistakenly think they can beat the enemy because they are smart. But you had better not get into any intellectual debates with the devil. "I have a 4.6 GPA. I've got a great mind. I've even read the dictionary from cover to cover." Not the *Bible*, mind you, but the *dictionary*.

You think that because you are intelligent, you can outwit and outthink the devil. However, you cannot outwit someone who has already seen every attempt at defeat from the beginning until now.

On your own, your mind does not have enough holiness capacity to outwit him.

DON'T EVEN THINK ABOUT IT!

Then the LORD saw that the wickedness of man was great in the earth, and that every intent of the thoughts of his heart was only evil continually.

(Genesis 6:5)

This very powerful passage of Scripture describes the Lord's anger and His desire to destroy the earth when the only thing on man's mind was new ways to commit sin. This passage also implies there is none of God's power available to help you fight the enemy if your mind is wrapped up in sin. *If you are going to have victory over the devil, you must get control of your thought life.*

Everything that becomes a habit in your life originally began as a thought. It started as a thought, which you eventually articulated, and after you said it, you acted on it. Note this, whatever you *say*, you are going to *have*. Why? The words that you speak are creative material, used as the ingredients for self fulfilling prophecies (Mark 11:23). Then, after you have acted on it, it becomes a habit which then becomes your character. So now you *are* what started as a *thought.*

That is why the Bible says you should be:

Casting down arguments and every high thing that exalts itself against the knowledge of God, bringing every thought into captivity to the obedience of Christ.

(2 Corinthians 10:5)

DO YOU NEED A PLUNGER?

What some individuals need is a *mental enema*. You may need someone to give you a spiritual Ex-lax because your mind is too backed up - it needs renewal.

His word gives us a whole list of things to think about so that our minds will not wander or be idle, or become clogged with the refuse of the world.

Finally, brethren, whatever things are true, whatever things are noble, whatever things are just, whatever things are pure, whatever things are lovely, whatever things are of good report, if there is any virtue and if there is anything praiseworthy - meditate on these things.

(Philippians 4:8)

Remember, "An idle mind is the playground of the devil." If you do not have anything good on your mind, the devil will give you something to think about.

THE SECRET WEAPONS

I can remember walking through *Borders* a while back, and in the midst of all of these great literary writings and spiritual texts by different people, I saw a section where they had "text books for dummies"; *Mechanic Work for Dummies, SAT's for Dummies,* etc.

That night I asked the Lord, "Lord, can You give me some *spiritual* strategies for dummies, for those of us who can't do spiritual warfare like Paul said?"

I do not mean to be offensive to anyone, but there must be some spiritual strategies for those of you who do not read the Book like you should, who do not pray like you should, who do not attend mid week teachings and Bible studies like you should; those of you who do not know the Word well enough to combat the enemy with it.

What if you are not smart enough, not astute enough to know how to fight the enemy on *your* turf?

What if you do not know how to put on the *right* armor to cover you and conquer him?

What if you have not been *saved* long enough to have learned the deceptive devices of demons?

What if your thought life is *out of control* and you cannot seem to pull anything together?

Good news, Friend, I have found some *secret weapons* that do not take much intelligence to operate – just obedience.

THE BLOOD OF THE LAMB

I found something very simple in the Book of Revelation.

And they overcame him by the blood of the Lamb and by the word of their testimony, and they did not love their lives to the death.

(Revelation 12:11)

In this passage, I saw a perfect strategy for dummies. You can overcome the devil if you can ***TESTIFY ABOUT THE BLOOD OF THE LAMB***. If you can just say something about the blood, if you can just *plead* the blood, you can be victorious. When you say, "I plead the blood," you are saying, "Lord, I want to put Jesus' blood over this area of my life: over my spouse, my children, my family, and my car, whatever!"

You may not know exactly what that means, but the devil does! Satan can still remember the time he saw Jesus, on the cross of Calvary. The Bible tells us that when Jesus hung on the cross, He was not wearing a robe or a loin cloth, all he had was a crown of thorns on His head and His blood all over His body. At first, seeing all that blood, the devil thought he had won.

But he soon found he was mistaken!

So when you say, "I plead the blood over my life," you are giving the devil a flashback of Calvary, and he remembered the last time he saw someone covered by Jesus' blood, he lost power!

So the first strategy for dummies is that, if you cannot quote an appropriate Scripture, if you can at least say, "I plead the blood", victory is on your side!

IN THE NAME OF JESUS

And being found in appearance as a man, He humbled Himself and became obedient to the point of death, even the death of the cross. [9]*Therefore God also has highly exalted Him and given Him the name which is above every name,* [10]*that at the name of Jesus every knee should bow, of those in heaven, and of those on earth, and of those under the earth,* [11]*and that every tongue should confess that Jesus Christ is Lord, to the glory of God the Father.*

(Philippians 2:8-11)

The next strategy is ***JUST ONE WORD, SAY, "JESUS."*** If you cannot even manage, "I plead the blood," you can still be victorious. Just get the word "Jesus" out of your mouth, and the demons will be forced to back off. This is the shortest and simplest strategy, yet the most powerful! This one 'name' terrifies governments and politicians. This one name has been 'banned' from public schools. Yet, it is the *only* name given under heaven that brings salvation to all mankind (Philippians 2:9-11). Come on, right where you are, ***SHOUT HIS NAME, "JESUS!"***

TELL IT LIKE IT IS… OR WILL BE

(As it is written, "I have made you a father of many nations") in the presence of Him whom he believed—God, who gives life to the dead and calls those things which do not exist as though they did; [18]who, contrary to hope, in hope believed, so that he became the father of many nations, according to what was spoken, "So shall your descendants be."

(Romans 4:17-18)

According to this text, God calls things that are not as though they are, and we are to do the same. In other words, the real battlefield is in our minds, because everything we are and do starts with a thought.

Rather than being scared to say something because you think the devil might take it, *you must say it* because you know you have the victory. Therefore, the third and final strategy is, you must have the ability ***TO SAY WHAT A THING IS,*** even if it is not a reality in your life yet!

Now the next day, when they had come out from Bethany, He was hungry. [13]And seeing from afar a fig tree having leaves, He went to see if perhaps He would find something on it. When He came to it, He found nothing but leaves, for it was not the season for figs. [14]In response Jesus said to it, "Let no one eat fruit from you ever again." And His disciples heard it. [20]Now in the morning, as they passed by, they saw the fig tree dried up from the roots. [21]And Peter, remembering, said to Him, "Rabbi, look! The fig tree which You cursed has withered away."

(Mark 11:12-14, 20-21)

Jesus' words to the fig tree and the dire results clearly explain that you shall have whatsoever you say, even if it is something negative. If you put your faith behind what you speak, then that is what you will have, good or bad (Proverbs 18:21).

The same mouth, energy and confidence that one uses to operate in faith, are the same ingredients used to speak and express fear! *You* control what you see by what you say. I remind you, *if you don't want to see it – don't say it!*

The old song of the church is still true: *(If you know it, sing it one time to encourage yourself)*

> *In the name of Jesus, in the name of Jesus,*
>
> *We have the victory*
>
> *In the name of Jesus, precious name of Jesus,*
>
> *Satan will have to flee!*
>
> *Tell me who can stand before us, when we call on that great name?*
>
> *Jesus, Jesus, precious Jesus, we have the victory*

Friend, when you cannot say anything else…say The Name!

PRAYER POINT

Father! Remove pride from my life and replace it with promise. In Jesus' Mighty Name, Amen!

SCRIPTURE REFERENCE:

Proverbs 16:17-19

Chapter Ten

The Secret of His Success

WHAT MAKES THE DEVIL SO SUCCESSFUL?

Recently I have been seeking, (not from books only, but from my own flaws, failures and mistakes, and by staying in the presence of God,) to try and find out what it is that makes the devil so successful. I must confess, learning how stupid I have been in relation to the enemy's tactics has caused me much frustration.

It was once said that if you want to hide something from someone, put it right in front of them. It is possible, even probable, for a thing to be right before you and you still miss it. In other words, it is possible for you to have the best parent(s) for *you*, yet not appreciate them. It is possible to sit in a classroom every day, yet flunk that class.

And it is entirely possible to experience something not just once, but repeatedly, and *still* fail the test the next time you come up against it. Therein lies the difficulty with dealing with the devil. Quite often though the truth is staring us right in the face, we cannot see it. And *that* is the devil's advantage.

WHY DO YOU DO WHAT YOU DO?

If you want to be a millionaire, you should hang around people who are millionaires and do what they do. If you want to have a 4.6 grade point average, you must associate with people who have 4.6 grade point averages.

However, if you merely desire to be average, befriend those with a 2.0 grade point average. If you want to be an imbecile, hang around with people who cut class. Whoever you associate with, you emulate. You pick up the attributes of whatever or whomever you are attracted or attached to. What is it that makes the devil so successful? What causes us to fall to him with such regularity? If you never ask the question, you will never find the answer.

First, you must discover why you do what you do. You must ask the right person, however, because you cannot get the right answer if you ask someone who is doing the same thing that you are doing. Instead, you need to ask your Manufacturer (God): "If I am made in Your image, why do I do these things that do not reflect You?"

I WOULD NEVER DO THAT!

The enemy can convince us to forfeit our future. He can persuade us to give away our virginity and our purity, our self esteem and self worth. He can get us to lie with such ease that eventually a lie comes more quickly and easily to our lips than the truth. We even find ourselves doing things or desiring to do things that at one time in our life we swore we would *never* do.

We lose our mores, our morals, and our scruples. Not only do we find ourselves doing things we never thought we would do, but we learn to justify our actions. And eventually we are in so deep that we do not care *who* knows what we are doing. Is that you?

HE'S A KNOWN FACTOR

Why is Satan so good at persuading us? It is not that we do not know his agenda, because as we studied in the previous chapter, the Scriptures clearly teach us that the thief comes only for the purpose of stealing, killing and destroying (John 10:10).

The thief does not come **except to,**

This means that if he shows up, his agenda is only those three things: to steal, kill and destroy.

We also learned that Satan does not have a vast arsenal from which to draw his weapons. He only has three: the lust of the flesh, the lust of the eyes and the pride of life (1 John 2:15-16).

God's word also tells us, that we already know these things about him:

...for we are not ignorant of his devices

(2 Corinthians 2:11)

WHAT DO YOU REALLY BELIEVE?

Yet, despite the fact that he does not have any new strategies and his weapons are very limited, and we know this; despite the fact that we have the blood of Jesus, the cross of Calvary, and a heavenly language with which to speak to God that the enemy does not even understand; despite *all* of these advantages, we continually become *willing* victims to his damnable delicacies.

Here is what you must understand: the moment you know the truth, not only are you now held accountable for what you know, but the devil then comes to see if you really *believe* what you know. Many feign ignorance because they do not want to be responsible for what they know. But even if you act like you do not know the truth, the fact that you have heard it still holds true.

Interestingly, as soon as I started teaching our local congregation about Satan's devices, the church started clearing out. Why? Because *the moment the devil is exposed, he can no longer use the trickery that he has already used for so long.* One of the greatest devices is his cognito! His success is his ability to be on the *scene* without being *seen*!

Neither He nor his agents can remain where his deceptive devices have been uncovered.

IT'S NO GREAT SURPRISE

So the great dragon was cast out, that serpent of old, called the Devil and Satan, who deceives the whole world; he was cast out to the earth, and his angels were cast out with him.

(Revelation 12:9)

It should be no surprise that we go *through* hell, because the devil *is* here, on earth. In the same way, if the devil is not in us, if he has been cast out; then woe to those who are around us, for they will end up with the devil seeking entry into them. He looks for the next most available *host* to continue his efforts of destruction! (Remember Mark 5:8-12)

And heaven is happy that he is gone:

Therefore rejoice, O heavens, and you who dwell in them! Woe to the inhabitants of the ***earth and the sea****! For the devil has come down to you, having great wrath, because he knows that he has a short time.*

(Revelation 12:12)

YOU'RE THE ONLY ONE FOR ME!

Notice the passage says,

Woe to the inhabitants of the ***earth and the sea****.*

The devil is territorial; he is possessive. He wants not only everything on land but everything in the water. Likewise, he does not just want you; he wants everything and everyone around you. The devil will try to convince you that you are the only one, but you must remember that he is a liar - he always wants *more*. So when He enters an individual…

He will never be committed; he does not operate in fidelity.

He is never going to be loyal to his spouse.

He will never be truthful with his parents.

Because once the devil has any area in you, he will always want more. If you give the devil a curfew, he will run over it. If you tell him to go *here* but not *there*, he will make you take it back. The devil is never satisfied staying in the area that you *give* him. You can not (I REPEAT) can not think that you can compartmentalize sin or its agents! My mom used to say, "Don't let the devil ride. If you let him ride, he's going to want to drive!"

ALL CREATURES GREAT AND SMALL

Woe to the ***inhabitants***...

In other words, every animal get ready, fish look out, the devil is here and things are going to be different. In the Garden of Eden, lions laid down with lambs. But look at all of the craziness we have today, Pit Bulls chewing up cats, and sharks attacking surfers. The devil has come down to earth - no wonder we have mad cow disease today! There were certainly not any mad cows in the Garden of Eden.

TIME IS SHORT

For the devil has come down to you, having great wrath, because he knows that he has a short time.

(Revelation 12:12b)

We should not be surprised that he is angry, that he has great wrath; *he knows that his time here is short.* Even though he has been here since Creation, he considers his tenure brief, and that is what makes him so effective; he disciplines himself not to waste time. What makes Satan so successful is that, he knows how to utilize time effectively and he does not try anything new; *he only does what he knows works.* He cannot afford to fail.

He does not branch out from his three main tools: the lust of the flesh, the lust of the eyes and the pride of life. He knows he has only a short time, so he does not try to accomplish everything. He is here only to steal, kill and destroy. He has reduced all his efforts into three easy steps to accomplish three easy results. It was five thousand years from the Garden of Eden to the cross. There are only about two thousand years from the cross to where we are now.

So for over seven thousand years, Satan has used the same weaponry, the same arsenal, the same agenda and it has worked. How can we, who have only seventy or maybe eighty years on this earth, afford to think that we can try new tactics and be able to pull it all together and accomplish victory, when the devil has had over seven thousand years and still operates as if his time is short?

YOU'VE WASTED HALF YOUR LIFE!

If you are fifteen years old today, you have already used up 1/5 of *your* life span. If you are twenty years old, you already dabbled into 1/4 of *your* life span. Those of you who are forty years old have now used up 1/2 of *your* life. So many of us waste the *best* years of our lives trying things and then have to spend the *rest* of our lives trying to recover from what we have tried!

IT'S TIME FOR A REST

Satan uses what has been working for over seven thousand years because it has proven to be successful. Many will try something once one night, on a whim, because their emotions are involved and they are hoping they can try it and get out.

Do the math: one night versus seven thousand years.

> *...one day is as a thousand years, and a thousand years as one day.*
> (2 Peter 3:8)

If a thousand years are a day, one night is not even a millisecond. Since it has been seven thousand years since Creation, we are actually in the seventh day according to the Lord's timing. The seventh day is significant because,

...*He rested on the seventh day from all His work which He had done.*

(Genesis 2:2)

Likewise, we also are to rest.

WICKEDNESS ABOUNDS

Everything ought to come easier for this generation than for any other. Truly, everything is easier because of the technology we have available, but the Scripture makes it abundantly clear that we have become increasingly wicked as we have hearkened to more and more of Satan's lies.

HE IS CULTURALLY SPECIFIC

The enemy is savvy to today's generation. What he used in the Garden of Eden was configured specifically for that *culture.* His tools were part of the cultural atmosphere: trees, fruits, vegetables, and animals. So Adam's and Eve's failure came through trees, fruits, vegetables, and animals.

At the time of Alexander the Great, however, he used the same strategy but different tools. Eve *saw* that the fruit could make her wise. Alexander the Great's temptation towards *the pride of life* was when he *saw* that he could own territory and be looked upon as a big man.

For each cultural atmosphere, the enemy configures his three arsenals, his three weapons, for whatever that culture is open to. Again, he has nothing new; he merely redesigns it for that cultural atmosphere in particular.

RECONFIGURED JUST FOR YOU

In my time, we had to "make love", just a cleaner term for fornication. In today's culture, it is simply "sex" - sex of every imaginable and unimaginable kind: girl on girl, boy on boy, whatever. That is today's cultural atmosphere.

You used to have to go pick up a woman on the corner for prostitution, now you can go online to send for an "escort" or merely virtual sex. You can log onto certain websites or visit chat rooms and pretend to be someone you are not. *Whatever your perversion, it is at your fingertips in cyberspace.*

The tools are no different; they are just reconfigured for the cultural atmosphere of our time. My grandfather used to make peach liquor out in the tool shed with a potato maker. Today's "tool sheds" are crack houses filled with crack and "ice". We take weed or whatever and wrap it up in leaves to make it look legal. *Same strategies, different culture.*

IT'S IN YOUR BLOOD

After the enemy designs his weapons for humankind in general and then reconfigures them for a particular cultural atmosphere, he then sits and watches the various bloodlines, in order to see what they are open to by virtue of the general nature of humankind and the specific cultural atmosphere in which they exist. Now it becomes more personal.

This is where we have come to deal with generational curses, because the enemy constantly monitors your bloodline and sees what your family has the propensity or a proclivity for. Remember, because he does not waste time and has a limited arsenal, he *studies* his "prey" no matter how long it takes, and calculates the best way and time to make his move. Then he *offers* that thing, whatever it is, to generation after generation of your family and he *presents* it to you individually.

WEAK AS DISHWATER

Once he has set everything up, he then *waits* for you to fulfill what he believes, by *faith*, is going to work. Yes, the devil has faith. He believes by faith that if he sets it up, you are going to fall into it every single time. That is why he does not have to do anything new.

He believes that your generational line is as weak as dishwasher, and that there is no one in it who will stand up and have enough courage in them to say, "Devil, the buck stops here."

Instead, he believes, every single one of you will continue to say, "Well it's in my generational line," and excuse the thing that you were supposed to expose. You then start making allowances for whatever God was trying to tell you to kick out. Truly, it is hard to expose what is in your generational line, in your blood, because *you* are the individual you see in it while you are trying to *hate* the thing that you see!

When that sin that you hate shows up in someone that you love, you must have enough God in you to confront the spirit and cast him out in order to save your bloodline. Many seek to minimize the activity of the devil in the world today and his activities as psychosis. However, as we stated in previous chapters, he *is* real, his presence *is* felt, and he *can* be evicted, by the power and the name of Jesus Christ.

CHOICES NOT CURSES

Once you become aware of that thing, though it is no longer a generational *curse*. Once you know it and still do it, it becomes a generational *choice*. You can choose your actions, but you cannot choose the consequences or repercussions. You cannot know how this thing will cause everyone in your family to turn out (even oneself) simply because it went a certain way for someone else in the family or a previous generation.

I call heaven and earth as witnesses today against you, that I have set before you life and death, blessing and cursing; therefore choose life, that both you and your descendants may live.

(Deuteronomy 30:19)

In other words, once you have heard *this* thing, (and it may be several things), was a curse on your family line and you still do it, you have fulfilled the *prophecy* that the *devil* had about your life, and set in motion a curse upon generations to come. His faith that you would be nothing more than your previous lineage has been fulfilled – by your choice!

Why? Because God was giving *you* the opportunity, the doorway, the power to break that thing by exposing it. However, instead of exposing or expelling it, you excused, exonerated it and embraced it. *There is power in choice.*

CHASING THE GHOST

There is no such thing as "I tried it once." One time sets in motion a whole generation of repercussions which you never even considered were going to come to pass.

The enemy only allows you to look at the tip of the iceberg, never to consider the long term. If you try something once, you have made a commitment for life. Even as you read this sentence, there are people out there who are trying something "one time", crack, weed, an illicit sexual activity or whatever it is, and soon they will be chasing that ghost forever. What is it that makes these things so potent the *first* time? It is not merely the thing itself, but also the purity of your system, emotions, mindset, etc.

Once you infiltrate your pure spirit with anything outside of the will of God, it is like injecting oneself with poison; you now have the strands of that pollutant in your spiritual "bloodstream".

But the high of that original loss of purity is what your being craves. So you begin trying to chase *that* ghost, and when you cannot get it, you start mixing other things in.

That is why rehab is ineffective for today's generation. All it does is give you thirty days, sixty days, maybe ninety days to feel pure. Once ones system is 'clean', back to its pure state, to do the same thing again tells your system it will feel like the 'first' time. But then you fall all over again, and begin the same fruitless chase. You do not need twelve steps, you need one step - *decide you are going to do what God is telling you to do.*

I ONLY DID IT ONCE

You can have sex just *one time* and still catch a sexually transmitted disease. Having sex just *one time* opens a door for the enemy, compelling you to sleep with anyone, anytime. If sex one time results in pregnancy, your life as you know it is over.

You can lose the best years of your life trying to recover from just one bad choice.

You must understand, however, that the issue is not just *the choice.* The real issue is *the time* spent in recovery. What makes the devil so damnable is not what he gets you to do, but the amount of time he gets you to waste your life doing it, and the length of time you spend trying to get out of it!

Time is precious, my friend, and you must learn to make use of it as effectively as your enemy. In the next chapter we will discuss timing - how critical it is to us and to our enemy.

PRAYER POINT

Father! Help me to, not only know my enemy, but also to know myself. In Jesus' Mighty Name, Amen!

SCRIPTURE REFENRENCE:

Romans 7:17-19

Section 3

SOARING TO HIGHER GROUND

Chapter Eleven

Timing is Everything

THERE IS A TIME FOR EVERYTHING

To everything there is a season, a time for every purpose under heaven: 2 A
time to be born, And a time to die; A time to plant, And a time to pluck
what is planted; 3 A time to kill, And a time to heal; A time to break
down, And a time to build up; 4 A time to weep, And a time to laugh; A
time to mourn, And a time to dance; 5 A time to cast away stones, And
a time to gather stones; A time to embrace, And a time to refrain from
embracing; 6 A time to gain, And a time to lose; A time to keep, And a
time to throw away; 7 A time to tear, And a time to sew; A time to keep
silence, And a time to speak; 8 A time to love, And a time to hate; A time
of war, And a time of peace.

(Ecclesiastes 3:1-8)

This is a familiar passage, telling us that there is a specific time for everything. There is a time to give birth - to bring forth life, and a time for death - when it feels like life is killing you.

There is also a time for embracing, when you need affection, and a time to refrain from embracing, when you need to push some people away.

Truly, timing is everything, and the Scriptures teach us that we must redeem our time, use it effectively, in these evil days (Ephesians 5:16).

THE MASTER OF TIME

As we discussed in the previous chapter, the devil is a master of time.

He does not waste time.

Humans, on the other hand, so often waste time caught up in sin, or in trying to recover years lost in previous sin. Meanwhile, the devil is always utilizing time to his advantage.

HIRING THE RIGHT BABYSITTER

There are specific ages and stages in our lives where the enemy is able to work more effectively. For example, psychologists tell us that a child's character is developed between the ages of one and six years old, and everything parents do from then on, until those children become teenagers, is merely directing what has already been established.

That is why screening the people you hire to babysit your child between infancy and six years old is critical. You cannot allow them to be sat down in front of MTV and let that television be their babysitter. Likewise, there is certain music that should not be played while your children are being nurtured.

There are some places you cannot take your children to and some people you cannot allow to hold them. No matter how nice they are, some people are carrying spirits that will transfer to your child, because children have innocent, open spirits. So be careful about who you allow around your child.

For the first couple of weeks, most people do not let anyone hold their babies. Why? Because everyone knows that germs may be transmitted from one person to another, and are especially harmful to infants whose immune system has not been fully developed. Well, keep in mind, if germs have that much authority and power, how much more authority does a demon have?

THE BABY KILLER

People thought that I was trying to be "uppity" when I did not want anyone around my babies. But that was not the case. I simply knew that at certain stages of their lives I needed to protect my children from certain people.

Notice that when both Pharaoh and Herod demanded the killing of babies, it was those from the ages of birth up until six years old. Today, Sudden Infant Death Syndrome (SIDS) only occurs in infants.

That same spirit that existed at the time of Herod and Pharaoh is still trying to kill your babies before they have a chance to come into being. Look at it spiritually. If you are an infant Christian, there are some things you cannot be around; there are some people you cannot allow to hug you; there are some places you cannot go.

These people, places and things have accumulated spiritual "germs" that can be transferred to you. It is the same with our children. We must protect them at all costs.

PLUNDERING PREPUBESCENCE

When children are moving into puberty, at ages of twelve to fifteen, there is a specific spirit that is trying to grab them. At this age, their bodies are changing; they are growing pubic hairs and busts, and are starting to become aware of their own sexuality. Just prior to this, they all look alike, flat-chested boys and girls.

Now, all of a sudden, they are starting to show differences. This is the age when children begin to identify their sexuality. It was at age twelve that Jesus surprised His parents by saying, "I must be about My Father's business". He was preparing Himself to withstand this spirit.

Jairus' daughter was twelve, coming into puberty, when she almost died. It is also at age of eleven and twelve that those who are sexual deviants, find our little boys and girls most attractive. And it is not a coincidence that young girls in junior high school, eleven and twelve years old, have now begun wearing little bracelets and are talking about "my girlfriend or my wifey"; and young boys are talking about their "boyfriends".

What is even more shocking is that their parents are merely letting it go. That same spirit that tried to kill Jarius' daughter is still at work today, trying to get a hold of our young people while they are in transition.

ADOLESCENT ANGST

It is at the ages of fifteen to seventeen, also known as adolescence, when children are at their wisest and brightest.

3Then the king instructed Ashpenaz, the master of his eunuchs, to bring some of the children of Israel and some of the king's descendants and some of the nobles, 4young men in whom there was no blemish, but good-looking, gifted in all wisdom, possessing knowledge and quick to understand, who had ability to serve in the king's palace, and whom they might teach the language and literature of the Chaldeans. 6Now from among those of the sons of Judah were Daniel, Hananiah, Mishael, and Azariah. 7To them the chief of the eunuchs gave names: he gave Daniel the name Belteshazzar; to Hananiah, Shadrach; to Mishael, Meshach; and to Azariah, Abed-Nego.

(Daniel 1:3,4,6,7)

Why did the king choose these particular adolescents, the individuals we know as Daniel, Shadrach, Meshach and Abed-Nego? It is because they were the best and brightest. Therefore those who could learn the king's language and run his kingdom. The enemy likewise, desires to grab our young people between the ages of fifteen and seventeen and convince them not to use their great minds.

Young adolescent men and women are ready to be intellectually stimulated. But why is it that so many fifteen to seventeen year olds do not want to go to school? So many claim: "School is boring. I can't learn anything".

Of course, it is impossible to think that *every* school is boring. Rather, it is a spirit trying to grab our young people. In Daniel Chapter three, the king decrees Daniel and the others must bow down to a golden statue every time certain music plays, betraying their God.

Not surprisingly, there is also a spirit, in the guise of music, that grabs our adolescent young people. Every time they hear "their type" of music, they "bow down to it" as well, and music brings an opening for sensuality and sexuality.

ENTERING MAN AND WOMANHOOD

From the ages of eighteen to twenty-one, young people begin to solidify who they are as men and women. It is quite interesting to see how society, with the enemy's influence, has it all set up. Beginning at age eighteen, you can do what you want without your parents' permission. At eighteen, you can get an abortion, you can get married, and you can join the military and get credit cards.

At twenty-one you can buy alcohol. You can do whatever you want without parental intervention, at just the age when you are about to make the most critical life altering decisions of your life. And as at the other stages, Satan is working behind the scenes, trying to destroy you.

Why? Because if you mess these years up, the enemy knows that you will waste countless years trying to get your life back together again. So he gives you every *opportunity* to make choices during this age from which you will never get a chance to recover. At age thirty, David came into power, fulfilling the kingly anointing on his life.

Likewise, Jesus at thirty was baptized and began His earthly ministry. The average individual at this age, however, is now starting to try to clean up the "credit choices" of their twenties. Most minds are nowhere near as mature as they should be at this stage.

THE END OF WANDERING

The number forty makes reference to the end of wandering. During Noah's time, it was at the end of forty days and forty nights that the rain stopped and the ark settled. After forty years of wandering, the children of Israel found their way out of the wilderness and entered into their promised land. Just when you are about to settle down into maturity, the enemy brings about a spirit at this age to make you regret what you had to go through to get here.

So then at forty, you start wanting what you did not have, and did not really miss, at twenty. New sayings have been concocted to justify the immaturity that many display in trying to "recapture" bygone days. "Fifty is the new thirty" and "forty is the new twenty". The reality is we are trying to make up for lost or wasted time, or recover from making bad or immature choices.

Society calls this the beginning of the middle life crisis. But in the spirit realm, it is merely part of Satan's plot.

MAKE A PLAN

There is a spirit for every age.

Satan gives you the opportunity to mess up at twelve, fifteen, twenty-one, thirty and forty so that the best years of your life will be spent trying to recuperate from the time that you have lost. That is why God makes it incumbent upon us as parents to give our children a plan.

Without a plan, our children are not going to have enough sense to know what to do at twelve or fifteen or eighteen. They need our help, because at age twelve, their hormones are going to kick in and at age fifteen, they will start wanting sexual things.

Without a plan, when they are eighteen and no longer need your permission, they are going to start getting twisted in their thinking. To combat the enemy's plan for our children, we must make a plan early and follow it, because life is certainly going to offer them another agenda. Young people have enough "friends". They need the adults in their lives to be mature parents.

YOU MUST ACT NOW

Recently while in a service ministering, I saw an eleven or twelve-year-old come up and throw something on the altar while I was preaching. Condoms. That baby knew that at twelve years old, she was experiencing something that must have come from someone else. She knew there is no way she should be feeling like she is feeling at twelve years old.

So she took advantage of the moment and she gave it up to Jesus. Likewise, you need to run to Jesus. If you wait too long, you will find that you are no longer sensitive to the things of God and you have missed your opportunity. You must act now.

PRAYER POINT

Father! Remove every area of procrastination from my life. Help me to use wisely the time I have been given. In Jesus' Mighty Name, Amen!

SCRIPTURE REFERENCE:

Luke 19:43-44

Chapter Twelve

Shake it off

ALWAYS BE PREPARED

Now that we understand the importance of timing, we must ask ourselves these questions: What is the secret of the enemy's timing? Are there specific times when we must be most watchful for the enemy's strikes?

The following passage contains the answers to these questions as it chronicles the enemy's attempt to abort the plan of Apostle Paul.

When it was day, they did not recognize the land; but they observed a
bay with a beach, onto which they planned to run the ship if possible.
[40]And they let go the anchors and left them in the sea, meanwhile loosing
the rudder ropes; and they hoisted the mainsail to the wind and made
for shore. [41]But striking a place where two seas met, they ran the ship
aground; and the prow stuck fast and remained immovable, but the stern
was being broken up by the violence of the waves. [44]And so it was that they
all escaped safely to land. [1]Now when they had escaped, they then found
out that the island was called Malta. [2]And the natives showed us unusual
kindness; for they kindled a fire and made us all welcome, because of the
rain that was falling and because of the cold. [3]But when Paul had gathered
a bundle of sticks and laid them on the fire, a viper came out because of
the heat, and fastened on his hand. [4]So when the natives saw the creature
hanging from his hand, they said to one another, "No doubt this man is a
murderer, whom, though he has escaped the sea, yet justice does not allow
to live." [5]But he shook off the creature into the fire and suffered no harm.

[6]However, they were expecting that he would swell up or suddenly fall down dead. But after they had looked for a long time and saw no harm come to him, they changed their minds and said that he was a god.

(Acts 27:39-41,44b; 28:1-6)

In summary, the text says that there was a storm and that the boat was wrecked. When they made it to land, Paul was gathering some sticks, and a viper grabbed hold of him. From this series of events, we can form a partial list of specific times when the enemy strikes.

THE SAME OLD SERPENT

The word *viper* makes reference to a serpent or a snake, and as we know from the New Testament, Satan is also referred to as a serpent:

So the great dragon was cast out, that serpent of old, called the Devil and Satan, who deceives the whole world; he was cast to the earth, and his angels were cast out with him.

(Revelation 12:9)

In Genesis, it was the serpent Satan used to speak to Eve, although the other animals must have also had the ability to talk. (Otherwise Eve would have been shocked when the serpent began to speak). Satan caused the serpent to speak so that Eve might think that it was her equal. However, while she was made in the image and likeness of who is above he was created in the image of what was beneath.

Notice it is always what is beneath you that tries to pull you down to its level

So the enemy is referred to as a serpent, not only in the first book (Genesis) but also in the last book (Revelation).

When we look at the Book of Acts, which is between those first and last books, we can concur that although the above passage tells the story of Paul and a viper, it is a type and representation of mankind and Satan.

IT'S ALWAYS GOING TO BE A SNAKE

According to the passage, the viper jumped and latched onto Paul's hand. This illustrates an important point about a viper. ***NO MATTER HOW WELL YOU TREAT IT, IT IS ALWAYS GOING TO BE A SNAKE.*** You can hold it gently, you can pet it, and you can treat it nicely. It can even seem to treat you nicely as well, but it still has the nature of a snake.

SORRY, NOTHING PERSONAL

I once heard a story of an old farmer who was out hunting in the woods when he saw a fire. As he rushed over and began to put out the fire, he found a badly injured old snake right in the midst of the flames.

The man felt so sorry for the wounded snake that once he had put out the fire, he picked it up, took it home and put it in his own little box with fresh grass in order to nurse it back to health. At first, the snake was so unable to help itself that the man had to catch mice and bring them to the snake in his box so that he could eat.

Finally one day, the snake had become healthy enough that the man was going to release it. But before he did, the man took the snake and held it to his bosom and said, "I found you when you were just about dead and I nourished you back to health, and now it pains me to have to let you go".

And while he was looking affectionately down at the serpent, the serpent reared back and it bit him in the face.

He threw the snake down and said, "How could you, after I rescued you, brought you back to life and fed you with hand-picked mice? You didn't have to struggle at all! How could you bite me in the face?" The snake turned and looked at him and said, "It wasn't personal, it's just in my nature". Then he slithered away.

ONCE BITTEN…

In the same way, there are some things that people are going to do to you simply because it is in their nature. They do not mean anything personal, they just have a curse on their life, or possibly on their family. That is why they do not feel bad when they do what they do.

It is simply their nature. If you have ever been bitten before (betrayed, turned on, etc.) do not take it personal. The problem is that, possibly, you were trying to cause an individual, by *your* actions, to be something he or she was never intended to be. They were never meant to be your friend; they were simply being who they are. *What they did was just a part of their nature!*

WATCH OUT! IT'S POISONOUS!

Have you ever considered the fact that, a poisonous snake has poison running throughout its own body without harm. Yet if that same snake bites you, the poison that does not harm it will kill you! Likewise, there are some things that other people can do, that will not affect them, but will kill you. They seem to be able to do those things over and over again and not feel guilty, never feel shame, or seemingly, never suffer any consequences. But not you.

Please understand, that serpent will put his venom in you and then go on about his business, leaving you with poison that is harmless to him but fatal to you.

Then *you* are left to spend the rest of your life searching for an antidote that is not available, trying to find a way to keep on living when you feel like dying, all because someone did one thing to you when you were vulnerable. Remember, that is what makes the enemy so effective: *his timing.*

DON'T STAND SO CLOSE TO ME

Prior to this passage, we find there were circumstances that led to Paul being close enough to the snake to be bitten.

But after long abstinence from food, then Paul stood in the midst of them and said, "Men, you should have listened to me, and not have sailed from Crete and incurred this disaster and loss."

(Acts 27:21)

What does this text mean to us in terms of Paul's experience with the viper? Obviously, Paul would not have been bitten if he had never arrived on that island. You cannot be bitten long distance. In order for the serpent to strike, you have to give it some time, allow it to get close, embrace it, invite it into your secret spot, and bring it into your confidence. *You cannot be bitten unless you get close.*

OUT OF THE COMFORT ZONE

Paul was attacked because he was *holding* the snake. How did he get that close in the first place? The history behind the text is that Paul was arrested and tried before Festus and Agrippa in Cacsarea, and was granted his request to stand before Caesar. So he boarded a ship to Rome with some other prisoners.

When winter hit, it was recommended that the ship stay in harbor, but because that area did not *look comfortable*, they decided to search for another place that did look comfortable. As a result, because they left the place they were supposed to stay in, they wound up having a shipwreck.

Listen, you may be on the verge of a snake bite when you would rather have what looks *comfortable* than that which looks *confrontational.* Let's look at a situation where comfort proved to be catastrophic.

YOU CHOOSE FIRST

Now the LORD had said to Abram: "Get out of your country, from your family and from your father's house, to a land that I will show you."

(Genesis 12:1)

So Abram began the journey with his nephew, Lot. When they arrived in the new land, however, there was a problem:

Now the land was not able to support them, that they might dwell together, for their possessions were so great that they could not dwell together.

(Genesis 13:6)

So Abram said to Lot, "Please let there be no strife between you and me, and between my herdsmen and your herdsmen; for we are brethren. 9 *Is not the whole land before you? Please separate from me. If you take the left, then I will go to the right; or, if you go to the right, then I will go to the left."*

(Genesis 13:8-9)

THAT LOOKS COMFORTABLE

The passage continues, telling us that Lot looked over at Sodom and Gomorrah - green, pleasant, well-watered - in other words, *comfortable.* The attraction of Sodom was definitely not its hospitality, however - remember that when the men of the city heard about the angels who had come to visit Lot, they did not come to offer their succor, they came to Lot's door saying, "Give us men that came here…"

…Bring them out to us that we may know them carnally.
(Genesis 19:5b)

Obviously that attitude had nothing to do with hospitality; it has to do with homosexuality. "Sodomy", the word for homosexual acts, finds its lineage in the activities of the inhabitants of Sodom and Gomorrah.

Let me just interject here, it does not matter how many laws are passed; it does not matter if you can put your partner on your insurance policy, homosexuality is *not* right in any shape, form or fashion.

Yet, due to His unconditional love, the Almighty God still loves the individual although He abhors the act. Our assignment, as ambassadors of Christ, is to administer the life changing love of Jesus to all mankind. If *this* is done, with the same grace extended that was given to us, then, even those in the grips of the world's hold will be set free!

RUNNING FROM CONFRONTATION

So although that area was known for its sexual perversions and immorality, Lot chose it. To Lot, the attraction of that well-watered plain was stronger than his revulsion for Sodom and Gomorrah. But we all know how Lot's story ends. You must be aware that sometimes the search for your comfort zone is what brings you into a storm. Trying to find the comfortable thing to do is what brought Paul into altercation with the serpent.

So many of us run every time something confronts us. However, when you leave what is confrontational because you want something comfortable, you open the door for the enemy to step in.

THAT DOESN'T LOOK FAMILIAR

When it was day, they did not recognize the land; but they observed a bay with a beach, onto which they planned to run the ship if possible.

(Acts 27:39)

The sailors decided that even though the land they saw was not a place they recognized, anything must be better than where they were. You know that the enemy is setting you up when you are not only looking for something that is comfortable and not confrontational, but when you will settle for something even though it is not familiar. You had better be careful when you choose something just because it is *different* from what you have.

My children used to say, If I wore something that was *not* a 'name brand' item, "Dad, you can't wear that."

I would reply, "Why not?"

They would answer, "Dad. You can't."

Once while I was out looking for some shoes. I was going to get some Timberlands, but then I saw another brand. I said to my son, "Hand me those." I did not consider purchasing them being a problem. They looked like what I was looking for and the price was less than I had planned to pay.

He said, "Dad, that's a New York shoe! Here in D.C., you're going to be set up if you put those things on".

"Set Up?"

I didn't quite know what that term meant. I had thought if you were set up, that was a good thing. My kids, who were updating me on the latest phrases and terminologies, let me know that being *set up* meant that I would start *attracting negative attention.*

So beware: whenever you have left where you were supposed to be and settled somewhere else simply because it was different or the *price is right*, you are on the verge of attracting some negative attention. You are about to be "set up".

IT'S GOOD TO BE GROUNDED

And they let go the anchors and left them in the sea, meanwhile loosing the rudder ropes; and they hoisted the mainsail to the wind and made for shore.

(Acts 27:40)

Most people are aware that when the anchor is down, it will only let the boat go but so far. But this boat's crew needed to lighten their load, so they left the anchors out in the water. They threw the anchors away and said, "Let it ride."

When you let go of your anchor, when you leave what was grounding you, you are on the verge of being set up. If you no longer have anything to stabilize you, when there is nothing to make you put on the brakes, you are headed for trouble. Something is wrong when your conscience does not bother you. When there is no one around to tell you that you are acting like a fool, when you are... *that you have gone too far.*

Beware when you are always the "sharpest knife in the drawer" and there is no one in your life who can call you in! Be concerned when there is no one that you will submit to. If no one can tell you anything, and *you* are your own authority, you are on your way to being bitten.

DOUBLE-MINDED, UNSTABLE IN ALL HIS WAYS

But striking a place where two seas met, they ran the ship aground; and the prow stuck fast and remained immovable, but the stern was being broken up by the violence of the waves.

(Acts 27:41)

In other words, one part of the boat got stuck in one place and another part tried to keep on going. *You know you are about to be set up, when in your own personality, in your own mindset, you are suddenly divided.*

You cannot figure out who you are, where you are, or what is going on with you. Whenever you find yourself being split like that, you are being set up to be bitten. You must be careful when your mind becomes so confused and under attack until you start to hear voices.

You were not made to deal with that kind of confusion. Whenever your life is confused, you are being set up. When the a waves of life keep crashing against the shores of your unsuspecting and fragile psyche, and you cannot seem to catch a break, the enemy is ready to launch his attack. He has been sitting back, watching your generational blood line, watching your choices, and setting you up to see if you are going to do what he expects you to do.

ESCAPED AT LAST?

The last part of Chapter 27 says something very powerful:

And so it was that they all escaped safely to land.

(Acts 27:44b)

All of that chaos happened, but *Paul still got away.* He survived everything the sea could throw at him, and it wasn't until *that* point that the viper came into the scene. The devil does not turn up the heat until he sees that you have escaped his original plan. It is only after you have survived various scenarios that would have taken other people out, that the devil knows he has to come closer.

After you have made mistakes and gotten out of them, the devil says, "I cannot let him get away now because I now know he is susceptible to me. So all I have to do is come in closer." The moment you survive those trials and tribulations, the enemy begins again, but *this* time he gets *intimate* with you.

NEW BEGINNINGS

That verse falls at the end of Acts Chapter 27, and fittingly, the number seven speaks to *closure*. The number eight on the other hand, speaks to one having a *new beginning*. The first verse in Chapter 28 tells us that Paul and the other passengers were ready for *their* new beginning:

Now when they had escaped, they then found out that the island was called Malta.

(Acts 28:1)

Remember, up until this point they did not know where they were, they did not know where land was, and they were being ship wrecked. Now they had escaped the storm, they had found land, and they had discovered the name of the island where they had landed. Often times, we find ourselves in a similar situation. We have survived the storms that could have, and in some cases should have killed us, and now we know where we are. We are ready for a new beginning.

You understand that the devil had access to your old life. However, since that old life is now closed and you now have a new life and a new beginning, you may not be expecting the enemy to still be either that close or that interested in you. *Therein lies the danger.* Just because *you* have a new beginning, does *not* mean that your adversary is going to throw away his agenda. He just works another way.

DON'T YOU WANT TO BE MY FRIEND?

It is at this point, when you are fresh in your new beginning, where you really need to be careful.

And the natives showed us unusual kindness…

(Acts 28:2a)

You can be sure the devil is about to strike *when people who have never been in your circle of influence suddenly start wanting to be your friends.*

Why does the relationship that I thought I would *never* have suddenly show up?

Why is *this* business opportunity coming now?

Why does that guy suddenly seem so cute?

Why can't you stop thinking about her?

Beware, the devil is going to get you by bringing people into your life that seem like they are treating you better. But the only reason it seems that way is because *you just came out of a storm.*

Everything looks good when you have just come out of a storm. When you have just had your thirtieth birthday and you feel like you do not have anyone, everyone starts to look good to you.

When you are turning forty and all of a sudden, someone in their twenties wants you, no matter who they are, they look good to you. Be careful when people all of a sudden start treating you extra nice; there is always a motive behind everything. Only time will reveal whether the motive is for your betterment or your detriment.

"Don't worry, I'll pay for it"

"Can I buy you a drink?"

If you just came out of a storm, it is not the right time to jump into new relationships. Instead, get out of those wet clothes, go take a bath, dry off and get warm. Give yourself some time to get your 'land legs' under you!

HE CATERS TO YOUR EVERY WHIM

...for they kindled a fire and made us all welcome, because of the rain that was falling and because of the cold.

(Acts 28:2b)

Those natives came and appealed to Paul's flesh, to set him up for that viper's attack. In other words, you especially need *to watch out for people who cater to just what you are feeling.* "It's got to be God because you knew exactly what I was feeling!"

Remember, the enemy sits on your generational line and watches what is happening in your bloodline. He knows the patterns of your parents and now your ancestral line *moves,* better than you know yourself.

What is it that your flesh is anxious for? What is it that is always on your mind?

Beware!

I THOUGHT YOU WERE MY FRIEND!

King David said, "*It was not my enemy who took me out; it was my friend, my confidant*" (Psalm 55:12-14). You need to be careful of those friendships that are just too friendly. Watch out when they whisper and their lips accidentally touch your ear, or they hug you and inadvertently brush against you sensually.

"Listen, if you ever need somebody to talk to, just give me a call. I know sometimes the pastor and leaders are busy. I'm here for you."

Wait a minute, when did you become such close friends? Sadly, some of the people who will pull you down the furthest are people that call you "brother" or "sister." In church, you drop your guard. You expect that those inside the doors are different from people in the world.

But when freaks, whores and liars *come through the door*, unless they have been truly born again, they remain freaks, whores, and liars. *Doors* do not deliver an individual, Jesus does!

The saying goes, "misery loves company." The truth is, spirits are attracted to like spirits. Remember my story about the carpet, the less people you allow in your home, the less footprints you have to contend with.

IT'S COLD IN HERE!

But when Paul had gathered a bundle of sticks and laid them on the fire, a viper came out because of the heat, and fastened on his hand.

(Acts 28:3)

As long as the sticks were damp, wet and cold, the viper was comfortable. While the sticks were wet, the viper could hide among them. So Paul gathered sticks and since the snake looked like a stick, he held on to the snake and carried it.

He did not realize he had something that he did *not* need because it was in amongst what he *did* need. Sometimes what you are using to comfort you actually has something in it that can destroy you, but you do not recognize it because it looks like what you need.

HE'S LIKE A FATHER TO ME

Maybe you grew up without knowing your real father, so the enemy sent someone into your life to take advantage of your need for affection.

This man is old enough to be your father, and he shows you some affection, tells you how beautiful you are, calls you "precious", and the next thing you know, you are giving him your body in gratitude.

Perhaps you lost your sister and you have been searching for sisterhood… and while you are looking, you end up in something that is *not* sisterhood because you are open for female relationship. This whole twisted mess does not happen because you *decided* to go that way, but because the enemy saw something in your blood line. The examples of how he plays on our pain and our past, and twists them with his perversion, are endless. This is why we need both the word of God and the power of the Holy Ghost to guide us daily!

He took advantage of good timing and twisted what you thought that you needed so that you could get bitten. Remember, the enemy knows your times and seasons. He is watching your bloodline and he uses what you are looking for and perverts it, so that you wind up using something deadly to comfort yourself.

ALL-CONSUMING FIRE

Notice it was not until Paul put the sticks on the fire that the snake even woke up. As long as you are cold and damp and unmoved, as long as you do not have any fire, no prayer life, no praise or worship, as long as nothing moves you, the devil will simply ride on you. Your normal everyday movement will not necessarily get a *rise* out of that dormant serpent.

Ah, but I dare you to get close to the fire!

The Bible says,

For our God is a consuming fire.

(Hebrews 12:29)

There are some things that cannot stay close to you if you get close to fire. Do not think that just because you plead the blood and holler the name "Jesus", that the devil will be happy to leave. Putting the enemy in the fire only makes him mad.

Once you get close to the fire, meaning establishing an intimate walk with God, the devil is going to wake up and attack you like never before. He will try and cause you to think that you will never get a job, that no one will ever want you, that you will never get free, and that your life is not worth living.

After you have been delivered, you will find yourself more pressured and more stressed because the devil does not launch his fiercest attack on you until he knows you have some fire for him. It is then that he realizes that his time is just about up! For someone holding this book right now, this explains the attack that you have been under for the past month. The devil is upset with the fact that you have refused to stop praising God, despite the affliction. My friend, let me assure you, *this* fight is just about over, in Jesus' Mighty Name!

DON'T COUNT ME OUT!

When the serpent jumped on Paul and bit him, he was on a superstitious island. The natives of Malta worshipped a variety of gods, one of which was named "Justice." So when they said,

No doubt this man is a murderer, whom, though he has escaped the sea, yet justice does not allow to live.

(Acts 28:4b)

They were actually saying that one of their gods must have sought vengeance on him. These same people, who had been so kind, who started a fire and welcomed Paul and the crew, now changed their minds and said, "This man is some kind of criminal." Isn't it amazing how people change their opinion *of* you when they can no longer do *with* you what they wanted to do?

It seems to me that "church folk" in particular have a way of bringing up the past. The moment that they know the testimony of your past, and you no longer need them as you did when you first came to Christ, they will then air the details of your past in a manner that will make others think differently about you. Obviously, this proves they never had your best interest in the first place. This is one of the deceptive manipulative characteristics of our *two-faced* adversary – the devil.

YOU ARE CUT OFF!

So as the Maltans were looking at Paul, they were actually preaching his eulogy, simply because he had *something* hanging on him.

But he shook off the creature…

(Acts 28:5)

That serpent had a physical attachment to him. He had to *physically* separate it from his flesh. So he shook it off. Likewise, there are some people you must physically cut off. You must make a physical separation of that fleshy relation. There are some people you cannot simply tell "It's over" you must cut them off completely.

You *cannot* continue as friends. You *cannot* talk it over. Your flesh knows that that individual has been is more than a friend, and if you try to pretend that you are just being friends, in a matter of weeks, you are going to be right back in the same situation. Even if it is not with that person, it will be with somebody with a spirit just like them.

You can no longer see that person as someone you have had a relationship with. You need to see them as a distraction, not your old "flame", but merely a result of a desire for comfort at a vulnerable time of need. Be careful of emotional soul ties that were birthed at points of pain, need, vulnerability or transition. These relationships are extremely difficult to get out of because of the timing and circumstances that created the *soil* of their growth!

INTO THE FIRE

But he shook off the creature ***into the fire****...*

(Acts 28:5)

Not only do you need physical separation from the creature, and to call it what it is, but you must also put it into the all-consuming fire of God! Whatever the devil has brought you; you must leave it in the hands of God. Instead of acting like you are strong enough to deal with it on your own, ask God to help you, you may have to pray, "God, when the phone is ringing, give me the strength not to pick it up when I see the caller ID".

There are some things you cannot stop on your own; you must put them in God's hands. Otherwise, all the devil will do is slow-walk you right back into the same old thing. Do not forget, the enemy does not come, except to steal, kill and destroy. Do you think he is going to have a distraction to your destiny to call you and say, "I'm calling you because I want to steal from you, to kill you or destroy you?"

Of course not.

The enemy is a liar. He will have to say things like "I love you. I miss you". But you must remember what that person is really calling you for.

MY BETTER HALF

Once you have shaken that serpent off, you can learn to be complete in yourself. You need to get to the point where you are whole by yourself so that you do not need someone to be your *better half.* If you are a half and you connect with another half, all you end up with is two broken halves.

Until you are complete in and of yourself, at peace with yourself and happy with yourself, you will never be able to compliment another individual…neither will another be able to compliment you.

PULL YOURSELF TOGETHER

…he shook off the creature into the fire and suffered no harm. [6]*However, they were expecting that he would swell up or suddenly fall down dead.*

(Acts 28:5-6a)

Most people who mess you up, turn you on, and then turn you out expect you to wind up just like them. They do not expect you to get yourself together.

There are those who assume you will fall apart simply because the marriage ended.

They expect you to fail just because you are a single mother.

They figure you will always be an addict just because you used to be one.

Listen, do not allow anyone to write your eulogy with the negative words or opinions that they have about you. You don't *live* by the words that come out of their mouths; you *live* by the words that come from the mouth of God!

KEEP WATCHING

…they had looked for a long time…

(Acts 28:6b)

The natives watched Paul for a long while, expecting him to swell up and die. They knew that viper's poison might take a while, but they were ready to wait. Likewise, the devil knows your time and your seasons.

Do not think that just because you said "no" to a damnable desire two weeks ago, that you will not have to say it again two weeks later. What you are weak to may not say anything else to you the rest of the year.

But don't fool yourself, next season at the same time, it will come right back again, and you will have to be as emphatic in your response the *next* time as you are this time. The enemy is willing to wait. It might not be the same person, but it will be the same spirit. *Please do not get hung up on the covering, it is the spirit that will come back again!*

I CHANGED YOUR MIND

Those natives really expected Paul to die. But after they had waited a long time and nothing happened, they finally changed their minds. And once *you* shake off that viper, there are a lot of people who are going to have to change their minds about you, as well. They will have to change their definitions of you.

They may have *known* what you were, but they will not know who you are. If you want people to stop knowing you from what you have been, then *change* what you are. *You cannot keep being what you have always been and then get mad when people call you what they have always called you.*

YOU DO NOT HAVE TO DIE

Those Maltans knew that viper had bitten Paul. They knew it had plenty of time, while it was latched onto his hand, to poison him. But he never showed any outer manifestations of the poison that had gone into him. *Listen, things that killed other people do not have to kill you!* Situations that messed up other peoples' lives do not have to make you lose yours.

Just because everyone else has a nervous breakdown does not mean you have to. Your marriage does not have to end. You do not have to lose your children.

You must decide that although you have been bitten, you will not die. You *shall not die, but live, and declare the goodness of the Lord* (Psalm 118:17,18).

You need to stand resolutely, while all of your enemies, the naysayers and complainers are looking at you expecting the worst, and say, "I may have been through some difficulties but watch me, I am *not* going to die. Take a good look at me, I'm still here. I may have been in a few rehab programs, been in and out of jail, been in a few messy situations, but *I'm still here.*"

If that is your testimony, congratulations, my friend! You are well on the road to *learning to soar*, and to living a victorious life.

Once you have shaken off the snake and your demons are defeated, what next? Can you sit back and relax for the rest of your life?

On the contrary, the Scriptures make it abundantly clear that preventative maintenance is in order.

In the next chapters we will formulate a plan for keeping your life *free* of demonic attack.

PRAYER POINT

Father! Thank You that neither storms nor serpents have been able to destroy me. I bless You that I am still here. In Jesus' Mighty Name, Amen!

SCRIPTURE REFERENCE:

Psalm 139:14-18

Chapter Thirteen

Get Moving

SNIPER ATTACK!

A few years ago there was a sniper out and about, killing people at random. He was in the Washington, DC area where I live. His deathly deeds were shown on the daily news worldwide. I remember, during that time, I took my wife and children out to celebrate Mother's day. When I was on my way back to my car, my daughter, who was walking towards her own car, said, "Dad, you're walking too straight, you are walking too easy."

I said, "What should I do?"

My kids replied, "move around a little bit."

"Move? You want me to walk down the street dancing or something?"

They said, "Dad, it's just that we don't want the sniper to get you."

YOU'VE GOT TO MOVE IT, MOVE IT!

Sometimes the devil has a bull's eye on you just like a sniper.

But I have prayed for you, that your faith should not fail; and when you have returned to Me, strengthen your brethren."

(Luke 22:32)

When you realize he has you in his sites, you need to move a little bit, shake it up. Let that devil know you used to be in one place, but you shook things up and you are not where you once were. As long as you let the devil, that snake, hang on you, you are not really alive. You have the potential, based on its attachment, to be a dead man. But once you shake it off, you can begin to live the life of abundance Jesus promised.

DO YOU HAVE ANYTHING GOING ON?

The enemy's greatest victories are not in the midst of storms but in *good weather,* when you have everything going well for you: a lucrative job, healthy relationships, good self esteem, when you know what your life's goal is, when you have a plan.

Why does he attack in the good times?

Listen, your adversary, the devil does not want broken down, useless people. He only wants people that have something going on. Then after he breaks you down, he leaves you alone.

CAN YOU STAND TO BE BLESSED?

Years ago Bishop TD Jakes authored a book, *Can You Stand To Be Blessed?* He wrote that if you need to have a lot of friends, someone you can call every time you are going through trials, someone who will always like you, then you are not ready to be blessed.

Being blessed is often a lonely process. Those who knew you before you were blessed stand back, watching to see how you are going to change. At the same time, the people in your new place of blessing do not know you yet.

Therefore, they keep their distance as well, leaving you *feeling* alone, abandoned or rejected, when in truth, you are in a *place* of blessing!

Sadly, some will never get to that place of blessing because they get so lonely in the process of obtaining it, that they end up forfeiting all the blessing in order to keep clutching what they had before. In other words, the discomfort of moving from what was comfortable (familiar) causes many to not move at all.

RUNNING THE RACE

If you have ever participated in a race of any sort, you will be familiar with the phrase "on your mark, get set…go!" But have you ever really thought about the meaning behind the phrase? Personally, I find it interesting to note that you cannot even be set and ready to go until you get *on the mark*.

What we are doing now is pressing *towards the mark* (Philippians 3:14), and when we get there, *then* we will know that we are 'set' and 'ready' for everything that God has for us. Some people run in Lane Three, some in Lane Two, some in Lane five, but their marks are all the same. There the analogy to a race ends, however, because in life we are not competing with one another - despite the fact that it often seems so. You are *not* called to try to be anyone other than who you are or to try to run in any lane but your own.

Therefore, you cannot allow what other people have or do to cause you to feel insecure. Nonetheless, breeding insecurity is one of the enemy's most common tricks – it so often seems that someone else's *sin* is bringing better returns than your *sanctity*. Not true! If you are truly going to shake the devil loose and move on from the place you are in, if you are going to run this race with success, *you must have a plan.*

You have to develop something new for your future. Otherwise, if you keep on doing what you have always done, you will keep on getting what you have always gotten.

TO KNOW ME IS TO LOVE ME

I spend a considerable amount of time trying to learn all that I can about God; I also spend a great deal of time observing people. Since we are made in the image of God and in His likeness (Genesis 1:26-27), it is nearly impossible to learn about Him, yet remain ignorant or oblivious of ourselves. In other words, *the more I learn about the One in whose image I am made, the more I learn about me.*

And in learning more about me, I then learn more about the people around me. My knowledge of God and my knowledge of self make me inextricably tied into a greater knowledge of others. The Bible even makes it clear that knowing and loving God and knowing and loving myself have a direct bearing on whether I can know and love you.

Then one of the scribes came, and having heard them reasoning together, perceiving that He had answered them well, asked Him, "Which is the first commandment of all?" [29]Jesus answered him, "The first of all the commandments is: 'Hear, O Israel, the LORD our God, the LORD is one. [30]And you shall love the LORD your God with all your heart, with all your soul, with all your mind, and with all your strength.' This is the first commandment. [31]And the second, like it, is this: 'You shall love your neighbor as yourself.' There is no other commandment greater than these."

(Mark 12:28-31)

DON'T THROW OUT THE OLD WHEN YOU BRING IN THE NEW

In this passage, the Lord Jesus was quoting from Leviticus 19:18 and Deuteronomy 6:4, 5. By quoting from the Old Testament, He is teaching us that we *learn from* the old while we are *learning* the new. In other words, you cannot merely take up a new walk with God and think that as a result of this new walk, you will not have to deal with some old things. Some of those old truths can give you new victories.

I LOVE YOU, BROTHER!

Anyone that is not *you* is your neighbor. Note this, how you deal with others that are not you is a direct indication of how you feel, not only about yourself, but about your God. In other words, if you are treating people a certain way, with a certain mindset, that tells a lot about how you feel about yourself and God. You cannot degrade your sister and say that you love yourself and that you love God.

You cannot lie and manipulate and still continue to say that you love yourself or that you love God. No matter how badly you want to act like, one has nothing to do with the other, the truth is that, if you cannot love your brothers and sisters, then there is something in you that you cannot stand about yourself.

If you cannot talk to your neighbor, then there is something broken in your communication with God. If you cannot work with other employees, then it must mean that there are some areas in which God cannot work in you. How you deal with others tells a whole lot about how you reverence God.

DON'T LOSE FOCUS

We have already discussed how the enemy sits back and watches our cultural atmosphere, and then presents to us, over and over, the one thing that will cause you to stumble, even though he has had no new arsenal or agendas for years. Yet sadly, even though we know his *modus operandi*, we are still susceptible to his weapons.

Over the years, I have noted how difficult it is for people to sustain anything of significance for any great length of time. It is amazing how quickly people become tired and bored and give up. They fall out of love in marriage. They lose their focus and then forget what their goals are. Some are unable to maintain their focus because of their culture, others because of their temperament.

Whatever the reason, when you are quick to lose focus, you end up making promises that you cannot and do not keep. Or else, you become so focused on yourself that you think you are *owed* something. This is exactly what the enemy hopes to happen.

TIME TO MOVE ON

Our attention span, according to psychologists and psychiatrists, is basically about eight minutes long. That's why the media offers us *sound bites* and cliché. So when it comes to sin, we do not generally remain in the same place for very long. When you get tired of one club, you do not stop clubbing, you just move on to another club.

For some, the same goes for any sin that they tire of. They do not stop sinning, they merely add something new to it. When you start getting bored with something, you are like a TV surfer. You flip the channel and then get interested in something else simply because it is new. You do not really want the *new* thing, it is just the newness of it that you desire.

Have you ever noticed how Hollywood pumps out the same story line over and over again, just with different actors or actresses? *War of the Worlds*, for example, was out years ago, but because this generation was not aware of it, Hollywood was able to dress it up, bring in a popular star to play the lead role, and attract a whole new audience to the same old movie. In the same way, the enemy keeps bringing the same old thing in a new wrapper.

He makes it look like a new thing, but in reality it is an old thing dressed in new veneer that is attractive to you. Remember, he has watched your generational line year after year, and knows what made your grandfather fall. So he presents you with that same thing that caused your grandfather to stumble, but he dresses it up so that it does not look like something your grandfather would have fallen for.

WHAT ARE YOUR SYMPTOMS?

When it comes to deliverance, I have come to the realization that I do not have time to deal with "fluff." Sure, I can medicate symptoms, but there will always be more. Rather than handle a myriad of symptoms, I need to recognize and deal with things at their root.

For example, if you are going to operate on my heart, but you give me the wrong anesthesia, one that I am allergic to, that means that the very thing that you were giving me to *take me under*, you now have to fight to keep from *taking me out!*

This means that now you are no longer working on my heart - the root problem, because first you have to deal with what almost killed me when you were trying to help me. We spend much of our lives working on symptoms instead of the problem, to the point that the symptoms *become* the problem. Then once we get delivered from the symptoms, the problem is still there.

The Bible calls the root problem a "strong man."

The whole time we thought we were solving out problem, we were merely working on the imps or the demons that are *easy* to get rid of, without dealing with the root of why we do what we do. *We never dealt with the strong man.*

GETTING TO THE ROOT OF THE PROBLEM

Anyone can pick the fruit of the problem, but if you want to get *rid* of that problem, you have to dig it up from the root. Many people struggle with getting to the root of things.

Getting to the root of an issue requires taking off *layers.* Taking off layers causes one to feel *stripped.* Being stripped causes you to feel vulnerable and *susceptible.*

Then, to get rid of that feeling of susceptibility, you get into relationships or other things that lead you right back to where you started. Many of us, I must confess are professional 'fruit pickers'. We are great at picking at this and picking at that, but we do not want to dig up the whole thing.

AN UNCOMFORTABLE WORD

That was the problem the Pharisees had with John the Baptist! They were so good at picking the fruit, but he proclaimed that the ax was being laid to the root of the tree, and the whole thing was going down (Mathew 3:7-10). John wore camel's hair clothing and ate locusts and wild honey. Obviously, he was not worried about trying to impress anyone. He did not even bother to try to sway the Pharisees in his favor because of their money or political power.

No, he merely told it like it was. He explained that God was uprooting them from their comfort zones by giving them a word that was uncomfortable. He forced them to deal with themselves in an unvarnished, unpolished, bare wood existence. Understand this, it was not a *'dressed up'* cross that Jesus hung upon. It was not beautifully polished or finished wood.

It was a splintered, rough piece of lumber. It was untreated. John proclaimed that God was stripping the Pharisees down until He could take the very thing that they were trying to avoid, lay them on it and let it crucify their flesh.

LET THAT THING GO!

That having been said, the difficulty with most of us seems to lie in, not getting delivered, but in *remaining* delivered, and holding on to what God has given us. Why do we have such a difficult time permanently letting go of those things we have placed at the altar? The problem is when you gave those things up, you failed to consider one significant factor: ***you have a responsibility to maintain your deliverance***.

When you come out of surgery, your doctor prescribes a certain diet and exercise program in order to aid in your recovery and to maintain the results of surgery. Likewise, once you have been delivered, you may need a *special spiritual diet*, to maintain that deliverance. Many are still struggling because they have not done any preventive maintenance. Once you are set free, there are things you must do to keep yourself free.

PUT YOUR EFFORT WHERE YOUR MOUTH IS

Many of those who get delivered experience a new joy, a new peace, a release that is unlike anything they have ever felt before, and then they swear to God (and anyone else who will listen) that they will never do whatever it was again. However, it is not enough to confess it with your mouth. It takes effort.

If you are not *doing* something different, you are always going to do whatever has been your routine. You will always do the thing that your body is accustomed to.

You have to plan to do something different. Many of us have sworn "I'll never do that again." Yet in a matter of days, in a matter of weeks and for some, in a matter of mere hours, we are right back where we said we would never be. We are right back in the same atmosphere that we claimed we did not want to be in.

THE MINISTRY OF RECONCILIATION

Sometimes, in order for a broken bone to heal properly, you have to re-break it. That is what reconciliation is, *the resetting of a broken bone*. It is bone that has grown back crooked and must be made straight.

In like manner, once you are delivered there are some things that look like they are all right, but in reality you are walking with a limp.

So now, you need to break something in order to fix it. You may be in a cast for awhile, but in order for you to get where you are trying to be, it has to be re-broken and *set* right, *"On your mark, get set…"* Remember, something was broken in the first place that got you into the mess you were in.

IS THAT ALL?

Why do alcoholics and addicts relapse?

Why does the sex addict seek out another relationship or revisit that familiar website?

Why does the abuser still lift his hand against his or her mate?

Why does the computer sex addict purchase new software?

Why does the codependent person suddenly start talking about how lonely he or she is?

Why does the controlling individual run from accountability?

Why is it that we set ourselves up for the very same thing that we said we no longer wanted to be? Is it because God did not do what He appeared to have done when we were in church shouting at the altar? Was it just an emotional expression with no real long term value?

After the altar, then what?

After you have *laid it down* on the altar, after you have given up jewelry and pictures of old love affairs; after you have written down names, have rebuked devils, have had oil and water poured on you and you have pleaded the blood; after all of that, what did you do differently?

Or did you merely do all of that and think that was all you had to do?

WHY DON'T YOU COME ON BACK HOME?

Why is it that the urge, the hunger, the appetite is so much stronger after you have done all of that, than it ever was before you did it?

When an unclean spirit goes out of a man, he goes through dry places, seeking rest, and finds none. [44]*Then he says, "I will return to my house from which I came."*

(Matthew 12:43-44b)

The reason one finds himself right back in the same mess again is because a docile, stagnant passivity gives the enemy an entry back into what he considers his home. In other words, you give the enemy permission to come to what he considers home, when all that has been done is the bare minimum and then one expects to sit back passively, waiting for God to come and do for you what you will not do for yourself.

CARRY YOUR OWN WEIGHT

It is a mistake to think that God delivers you and then you have no responsibility. It is a trick of the enemy. Even Jesus had to carry His own cross, and He said those who would reign with Him are going to suffer with Him as well. If you do nothing to fortify what you have been delivered from, then you are going to find yourself losing a fight that you were never supposed to have fought in the first place.

Remember in Mark 5:38-42, the Master came to the home of Jairus and delivered his twelve year-old daughter from a sickness that had kept her listless and lifeless. Yet after the breakthrough, His first command was to tell no one and then *give her something to eat* (v 43)! There must be an effort on our part to maintain the deliverance or "feed" it, lest we find ourselves relapsing into what God miraculously got us out of.

JUST DO IT

Brethren, I do not count myself to have apprehended; but one thing I do, forgetting those things which are behind and reaching forward to those things which are ahead,

(Philippians 3:13)

Maintaining your deliverance is something that you *do*. You must make an *effort*. If you sit back and say that you cannot do anything, you are lying, and all you are doing is setting yourself up for the enemy to come in and take more control. You must declare over your body "Off Limits!" to your old habits. Declare over your flesh, "No Vacancies". Your body is the temple and the dwelling place of the Holy Ghost of God. You must let the enemy know, in no uncertain terms that you are going to glorify God in your body and therefore, he is not welcome.

Persona non grata is a term I learned in history class. When a foreign government did not want a particular diplomat to have access to their country, they would consider that person as "persona non grata", which means fully unacceptable or unwelcome. You need to give the enemy and every former habit *persona non grata status* in your life.

Until you do, until you let the enemy know, "you are no longer welcome here", and then move from that spot, he is going to think that he can always come right back there again. Tell every negative attitude and mindset that your body has the Holy Ghost living inside, so that you will not have these unnatural *unholy spirits* inside of you.

You cannot serve God and them. You cannot have both things in your life and claim that you love God more than anything. E.A Adeboye of the Redeemed Christian Church of God states, "Heaven and Hell cannot coexist in the same arena."

PROACTIVE, NOT REACTIVE

It is so important that you understand that you have to do something. You must be *proactive* as opposed to *reactive*. Many of us wait until something happens and *then* decide we need to do something. We react. And what blows my mind about Christians is that, it is not that we do not know what to do. We all say "I know what I need to do". So the problem is not knowledge.

Not only are people destroyed for a lack of knowledge (Hosea 4:6), they are doubly entrenched because they are destroyed by a lack of *not doing* what they *do know*. It is not that you do not *know*, it is that you do not *do*. Some have been in church long enough that they should be starting church by now. They have enough "insights" to be teaching seminary.

You ought to have so many ministries bursting out of you! Why is it not happening? For as long as you were *on* drugs, *dealt* drugs, *sold* drugs, *smoked* drugs, and now have been delivered *from* drugs, you mean to tell me you cannot run a drug counseling center? Why is it that you have not done it? It is because it is not enough just to know it; *you have to do something with it.*

A LIE FROM THE PIT

God shared with me that, *"one sinful lie was made up of energy-induced perversions resulting from active manipulation and deception, thoughtful weeks and months in advance, with a well-defined goal."* So once one gets delivered from the activities, He said for that individual to think that he was not going to have any energy to be able to do what God told him to do was a lie from the pit.

Listen, if I previously spent my energy *thinking* up lies, I now have to *plan* to tell the truth. If one's life was full of late-night street running and bed hopping, they would now have to fill their late night with some *positive* activity to counter what they used to be doing *negatively*.

Let him who stole steal no longer, but rather let him labor, working with his hands what is good, that he may have something to give him who has need.

(Ephesians 4:28)

You have got to do something.

PLAN IT OUT, STEP BY STEP

If you are trying to get delivered from some lifestyle or get into a relationship with God, you must think weeks, months, and even years ahead of time. Plan what you are going to do, and walk every step that it takes to get that goal accomplished. What is your ultimate goal?

Why is it we have so much wisdom when it comes to the things of the world and then seem so hopeless when it comes to the things of God? If you can plan a lie, look right in someone's face and tell it convincingly, how dare you proclaim you cannot evangelize! How dare you state you cannot witness about Jesus Christ!

HOW DO YOU LIKE ME NOW?

So many people get delivered and then say, "Well, I don't walk the way I used to walk." I do not care about how you used to walk; I want to know how you are walking now. You cannot get delivered and say, "I just stay in bed. I just watch TV." If you think this is going to keep you free, that is ridiculous.

You have energy stored up from the sin you have been delivered from. So you cannot just stay in the house, lie in bed and talk about how you do not sin anymore. If you do nothing with the 'free time', now you are wide open for something new to come in.

PENT UP ENERGY

It happened in the spring of the year, at the time when kings go out to battle, that David sent Joab and his servants with him, and all Israel; and they destroyed the people of Ammon and besieged Rabbah. But David remained at Jerusalem.

(2 Samuel 11:1)

There is a season for fighting and there is a season for renewing your strength. The scriptures tell us that kings went out to war in the spring of the year. In other words, all fall and winter they planned out their strategies and renewed their strength. But when the spring of *this* year came, which was the set time for battle, David decided, "I don't feel like fighting." So he stayed in bed, and the energy that he had stored up all winter long made him restless.

After he had sent everyone else out to fight, he got up and did something very innocent; he went for a walk on his porch. There he saw a woman bathing down on the porch beneath him. All the energy he has stored up for fighting was twisted into energy to create a *strategy* to get this woman and put her husband in danger of death on the front line.

Because he was not where he was supposed to be, doing what he was supposed to be doing, he used his scheming ability, reserved to create strategies against enemies, to do something that he was never supposed to do.

WHAT DO YOU HAVE ON YOUR PLATE?

The enemy uses you at the time when you are supposed to be fighting. That is why I do not understand people who allegedly have so many things on their plate, yet they still find time to sin. If you have *that* many things on your plate, you ought not to have time to do anything but go to sleep from exhaustion.

Ones inactivity in the things of God is an opening into being active in the things of the enemy. He tricks you into you thinking that there is nothing to do. "The church doesn't have anything to offer." "I don't have any friends." That attitude is birthed in selfishness and held together by the glue of the pride of life thinking that the whole world ought to revolve around you. It is the sound of one who has a 'restless' spirit.

GET ACTIVE

You ought to be active in some area of ministry in your local assembly. If there is not an area that suits you, *create one.* I know you can be creative because some of the areas of sin and depravity that the Almighty had to deliver you from, *you* created. Some of the lies you told, so that nobody would know who you were dating, you created.

And now you are trying to say you cannot create a ministry? Believe me, you have creativity in you, you are just using it for the wrong god. Once you get delivered, you need to get in everything happening at your church, in a charitable organization or on the mission field. If nothing is going on, then you should be the one that starts it up.

Then the real struggle begins: "I really don't want to start something, but I'll work with somebody." Yet, the very thing that caused you to fall was somebody who, as you put it, *pulled you in.* Well if somebody pulled you *into* sin, you ought to now with your new walk with God, start pulling someone out.

Do not be a follower any longer!

PRAYER POINT

Father! Deliver me from spiritual lethargy and apathy. Give me a fire that will not allow me to be complacent. In Jesus' Mighty Name, Amen!

SCRIPTURE REFERENCE:

Ecclesiastes 9: 10

Chapter Fourteen

Preventative Maintenance

YOU'VE GOT TO SERVE SOMEBODY

There was a folk song years ago by Bob Dylan called, "You Got to Serve Somebody". The song says, "you may be a king that's sitting on a throne or you may be a pauper that's sitting all alone, but you're gonna serve somebody." There is much truth to that song. You were created to serve God and subdue the earth. You must understand that the nature of man is to work.

If a man or woman will not work, then he or she is not supposed to eat! (II Thessalonians 3:10) There *are* circumstances where some individuals *cannot* work. I am not referencing them. However, if an individual is able, but *will not* work, he should not be patronized nor sympathized. Likewise, if one has experienced God's grace, but will not be productive in the kingdom, he should be 'cut off'. (Luke 13:6-9).Understand, if you are not working for God, you are working for the enemy. How so? *Inactivity* in the kingdom of light is *activity* in the kingdom of darkness. *There is no neutral ground!* (Matthew 12:30)

Although God is long suffering and kind, to continually claim deliverance but still go on in the same area of sin makes a mockery of His grace (Romans 6:1, 2, 6). It makes Him look impotent, and He is by no means impotent.

To keep on having to come back more and more and more, not for a new thing but for the same thing, tells the devil that you think you are stronger than God in this area. Why? Because we have not completely released the control of that particular area over to the power of God.

I'M SORRY, SO SORRY

I know that after you mess up, you are really sorry, and I know you are sincere when you confess, "But this time, I promise."

The murderer is always apologetic when he is about to get the electric chair.

The unfaithful spouse is always remorseful when his wife says, "I won't put up with this for one more day."

The alcoholic and the addict are always sorry and they swear with tears after they have relapsed again.

Why is it that our wisdom does not kick in until *after* the damage has been done?

What if we would have put up some barriers?

What if we would have set up some standards?

Sadly, we learn our lessons after the fact.

NO SECRETS!

One young lady I talked to, started out being raped by a man when she was sixteen. Now she is forty-nine and *living* with the same man, raising *his four* children. What she claims she hated, she never confessed, exposed or put up barriers to keep from indulging in or entertaining. Because of this, unbeknownst to her, she kept the door open for *that* spirit to think that it could always stay there.

I feel no regret, after extensive counseling, telling her that there is nothing I can do for her because *she* has not decided she is sick of the situation. The devil tries to make you ashamed to tell. He tries to make you keep it secret. He tries to make you manipulative and deceptive. Remember this; as long as you do not tell, and protect his presence through denial, you give him *freedom* in dark places.

The devil loves to be in dark places, but the moment you expose him, then you can get him cast out of you. Why? Because *God cannot heal what one will not reveal! If you can expose it, He will expel it!*

AFTER THE FACT

It is a shame that we do not recognize our downward spiral until after the life of some innocent boy or girl has been ruined, until after you have damaged your college opportunities. When you were in eighth grade you did not see the damage that would be done if you followed what everyone else did, acting cute and funny, hanging out, and getting high. Now it is too late. Why couldn't you listen to what somebody was trying to tell you, or by looking at the lives of other people?

I PASSED THAT OPPORTUNITY BY

One of my deepest regrets in life is passing by an opportunity to break away. When I was in middle school, I had an opportunity to be a member of the first graduating class from a new school in the city, Ellington School of the Arts.

My teacher believed in me and told me that I could do it. But when I had an opportunity to leave, I told myself that I did not want to leave my friends. So I let the opportunity pass me by. What was the problem? Was it my friends? No, it was not my friends. The problem was I had to ride a bus from where I lived in order to get to an area that was unfamiliar, and I had never ridden a bus, to any place that was that far away before.

The fear of the unknown (a new school unfamiliar surroundings, a mode of transportation I had never experienced) coupled with a lack of encouragement to take that ride across the town, caused me to move no further than my immediate neighborhood… So I ended up not going to school. The next thing I knew, I graduated from high school and was working at a barbecue restaurant. *This was not where I saw myself.*

This was not a career move, but it was where I was, with no way out in sight. Why? Because nobody told me how to overcome my fears and insecurities, I lost out on some college opportunities. *Do not miss your opportunity*. Do not miss a chance for a better life simply because you have fears and you are running from those who would tell you how to overcome them.

A CHALLENGE TO PARENTS

I want to challenge every parent reading this text to push their children to go farther. Tell them, "You need to leave this area. You need to get out of the house. You need to go to a school in another city." Do not be afraid. Encourage them to go far. If you do not, they will not go at all. I wish somebody would have pushed me. I know I had my fears and insecurities, but I wish (looking back retrospectively) "I had known then what I know now." How many times have we all sung that sad song?

If you never go any further than where you are, you are only going to have where you are to choose from. That is why an individual keeps choosing the same types of men, those types of women, those types of houses, jobs friends and so forth, because they do not know anything better. Why? Because they have not been exposed to anything different.

It is like fishing in a bucket. We *must* be stretched to another level if we expect to break the mold of normalcy off of our lives. You are creating and recycling the same thing that your community has become.

TAKE RESPONSIBILITY!

Most of us learn our lessons after we have messed up someone else's esteem and lost our own. And no, this is not a generational curse. *Generational curses were not illustrated in the Bible for the purpose of giving you someone to blame.* The truth is you simply refuse to take responsibility.

What kind of madness is that?

It is a sad state of affairs that in this day and time, no one promotes taking responsibility. Everyone promotes blaming something or someone. Your psychologist wants you to look back at your childhood and your parents, and place the blame there. But there have been many people who have been in much worse, much more tragic situations than most of us, and they still turned out to be product, successful assets to both society and the Kingdom.

They have been molested and raped or abandoned or passed from foster home to foster home, yet they still turned out to be examples and role models or mentors. It is no one else's fault you are where you are. Maybe you cannot do anything about what has been done *to* you, but you certainly can do something about what *you do* from here! Placing blame is not a new phenomenon. In Genesis, no one wanted to take responsibility. Adam blamed God and Eve. Eve blamed the serpent.

Here is where the true generational curse began. The real generational curse is not alcohol, not drugs, not sex or any other outside stimuli or family dysfunction. If you want to know the *real* generational curse; it is *blame.* It started with the Adam family! Many act as if they are the only ones who have ever had a child out of wedlock, or that they are the only ones who have ever had a broken heart. You may have had that happen to you, but what have you done since then?

DON'T PLAY THAT BLAME GAME

After Adam and Eve sinned and refused to take responsibility, Eve eventually gave birth to Cain and Abel. When Cain was confronted for killing his brother, he started playing *word* games with God. "Am I my brother's keeper?" (Genesis 4:9)

Once you as parents do not kill something (in this case, "blame"), it becomes *arrogance* in your children, to the point that they will even stand up against not just you, but God.

When you did not confront the issue in them, an *undealt-with spirit* will always progress, becoming more and more prominent the longer it can continue to run its course unchecked.

Adam spent all his time tilling the field. I can imagine he was mad at Eve. He blamed her for how hard he had to work in order to get what they needed. He was not used to work this hard.

Now, he had to live by the sweat of his brow, and he blamed her instead of blaming himself. *If only he had spoken up*. If only he had confronted the serpent. But he remained silent.

Now he has to get by *perspiration* what God was giving by *inspiration*. Adam was so busy working that he left Eve to run the house and raise the boys.

His absence aided the spirit of compromise and blame, and caused a rift between the boys, Cain and Abel, and between Cain and God Hence, Cain's anger at God caused him to kill Abel and feel no remorse. This is the next level of blame.

YOU MAKE ME LOOK GOOD

Where do wars and fights come from among you? Do they not come from your desires for pleasure that war in your members? 2You lust and do not have. You murder and covet and cannot obtain. You fight and war. Yet you do not have because you do not ask. 3You ask and do not receive, because you ask amiss, that you may spend it on your pleasures. [4]*Adulterers and adulteresses! Do you not know that friendship with the world is enmity with God? Whoever therefore wants to be a friend of the world makes himself an enemy of God.*

(James 4:1-4)

If I know that you have a future and a hope, and I do not have one, if I can connect with you, I am bringing you down, which means I am fighting against your goal. Many of us befriend people because they make *us* look good rather than because they are good for us. There are so many people who are no longer in our lives whom we claimed we loved.

But we did not really love them. There may have been some attraction, lust possibly or admiration, but not "love" in its truest sense. They were simply people whom we thought we would never get or maybe never have been another chance with. It was never real love, otherwise, why was it not maintained?

RIGHT STUFF, WRONG MOTIVE

God declares the problem is not that He does not hear your prayer, but that you have been asking with selfish motives. You only want to be blessed so that you can have an easier life,

...that you may spend it on your pleasures.

(James 4:3b)

You only want Him to give you the relationship because you want someone to pay your bills, take care of you, give you security and companionship.

However, you never even mentioned that you wanted the relationship because two are better than one and together you could bring more glory to God through a sanctified marital relationship.

These criteria can be used for anything that we seek God for. What is the motive? How do God and His kingdom get glory out of our request? The fact that you never asked for what you wanted for the *right* reason, could be why He did not give you what you asked for. Listen, if He blesses you when you have a perverted plan, then it will look as if He blesses perversion.

WHAT'S THE REAL REASON?

Look at your motives behind everything. Why do you want *whatever* you desire? You name it. Is it because you really *need* it or is it to fulfill something *in* you. Is it to prove a point to someone else? Are you competing with someone in your age group? Is your desire to advance the agenda of the Almighty? Let's be honest.

We thank God for our sons and our daughters, but let's get to the root of it. Why did we really have them? Was it really a plan to have them, or were we trying to prove something or make someone stay, and we got something we did not bargain for? God desires truth. If you never deal with the real truth about why your children are here, you can never love them purely.

THE REPLACEMENT CHILD

When Eve lost Abel, she was emotionally damaged. Adam came in from the field long enough to go into his wife again and produce another child, whom Eve named Seth. Interestingly, Seth's name means: "The Lord has given me a man child, in place of the one I lost."

In other words, all Eve wanted was a baby to make up for the one that she had lost. Which means that Seth never really got the love of being "Seth." An individual love. He only got love that Eve had wanted to give to Abel. The name "Seth" means a *substitute* for something else.

Every time Eve called his name, she was saying "Substitute; not my original choice; not what I really wanted, alternate for your brother."

She named him something that he would have to carry throughout his life ...*he was not really wanted for who he was!* How many people have you damaged because they were taking the place of an ex-lover who went out of your life? Though you said you loved them, somehow they always felt like they were not the most important one.

SUBMIT TO GOD

Therefore submit to God.

(James 4:7a)

The first step of preventative maintenance is: ***GIVE GOD COMPLETE CONTROL OF YOUR LIFE***. If you do not want to lose what you have, you must give God complete control of your life. That means, you have to surrender.

In all your ways acknowledge Him, And He shall direct your paths.

(Proverbs 3:6)

SET A STANDARD FOR HOLINESS

Resist the devil and he will flee from you.

(James 4:7b)

Step two: ***YOU MUST SET A STANDARD FOR HOLINESS IN YOUR LIFE***. The only way to resist the devil is to maintain a standard for holiness. You need to know that the enemy does not stay away just because you hurt or just because you are "serious this time." He stays away when you live holy. It is only holiness that he steps back from, not "I'm just trying to do the best I can."

The Bible says,

> *Therefore you shall be perfect, just as your Father in heaven is perfect.*
> (Matthew 5:48)

God does not ask you to be something you do not have the ability to be.

Stand fast therefore in the liberty by which Christ has made us free, and do not be entangled again with a yoke of bondage.

(Galatians 5:1)

DRAW NEAR TO GOD

Thirdly:

Draw near to God and He will draw near to you.

(James 4: 8a)

YOU MUST BECOME DESPERATE IN YOUR RELATIONSHIP WITH GOD. In other words, you have to fight your way back in to get close to Him, because the relationship is not what it once was.

As the deer pants for the water brooks, So pants my soul for You, O God.

(Psalm 42:1)

You have to want this relationship so desperately until you will "pull out all the stops" to maintain it. Your relationship with God is a matter of life and death. I have always told my children that for every area of their lives, they must set a standard, they must develop criteria for the people they want in their lives: friends, acquaintances, boyfriends, girlfriends, even jobs.

Whatever it is that you say that you want, *set a standard.* When you are dealing with people, your first criterion must be that they love God more than they love you.

If they love you more than they love God, they will let you get away with things you need to be confronted with. You need someone who loves God enough to say, "You know what? I love you but you are messing up, your anointing is going, you are living a life that's shallow."

***You need someone in your life who loves God so much so that they will sacrifice their relationship with you before they let you sacrifice your commitment with God*!** What a pity that most of us do not have people in our lives like that. We have those who *need us* to validate them, so they say what we want to hear.

CLEAN UP

Next,

Cleanse your hands, you sinners; and purify your hearts, you double-minded.

(James 4:8b)

Cleansing your hands makes reference to working and activity. This speaks to the purity of why you do what you do. It speaks to your motive for moving. ***YOU MUST REFRAIN FROM ALL OUTWARD SINFUL ACTIVITIES***, because sin is open rebellion against God and His Word. Once you have become desperate for Him, there are certain things you are just not going to do.

Abstain from every form of evil.

(1 Thessalonians 5:22)

Some activities might not be wrong but they sure do *not* look right. If you are a single man or woman, it would not be wise to be taking someone that you have a sexual affinity for into your bedroom saying, "We're going to pray." That might really be your plan, but it does not look right.

You need to know that what became a *hard-to-get-out-of-situation* did not start out being difficult to walk away from.

You have got to purify your heart and no longer be double minded. You must rid yourself of what you want and *fill* yourself with what God wants.

Your kingdom come. Your will be done On earth as it is in heaven.

(Matthew 6:10)

You must hate what God hates and love what God loves, hold on to what God says to hold on to, and let go of what and who God says to let go of.

Create in me a clean heart, O God, And renew a steadfast spirit within me.

(Psalm 51:10)

REPENT!

Lament and mourn and weep! Let your laughter be turned to mourning and your joy to gloom.

(James 4:9)

You must now repent. You cannot regret the fact that you are not getting blessed; ***YOU MUST REGRET THE FACT THAT YOU HAVE OFFENDED GOD***. Real repentance is not just saying “I’m sorry because I’m not getting blessed”.

It is, “I’m sorry, God, that I offended your law.”

Most of us do not regret what we’ve done. I used to say, “I don’t have any regrets because it took everything that I’ve been through to make me who I am.”

God convicted me on that. Is who I am who He designed me to be, or am I a product of the things that I have done that

I should have regretted? I may have made the best of a bad situation, but I want to know what I could have been. What could I have become? What could I have been, had I not done what I did?

For godly sorrow produces repentance leading to salvation, not to be regretted; but the sorrow of the world produces death.

(2 Corinthians 7:10)

Whenever I have godly sorrow, I am working on my salvation and I should not have regrets. The only time I should have regrets is when I do not have godly sorrow.

HUMBLE YOURSELF

Humble yourselves in the sight of the Lord, and He will lift you up.

(James 4:10)

This is the hardest one. ***YOU HAVE TO FIGHT TO KEEP FROM THINKING THAT YOU ARE STRONGER THAN YOU REALLY ARE.***

Therefore humble yourselves under the mighty hand of God, that He may exalt you in due time.

(1 Peter 5:6)

A lot of us pray, "Lord make me humble."

But God says "I can't. I can *keep* you humble but I can't *make* you humble. Because you have to humble yourself. Once you humble yourself under My hand, I can keep you there. But I will not grab your high-minded self and pull you down."

God is not going to make you humble.

If you do not humble yourself, however, you will set yourself up for *circumstances* to bring you down.

Pride goes before destruction, And a haughty spirit before a fall.

(Proverbs 16:18)

Some of our public humiliation is because we had secret pride and thought that we were stronger than we really were. Hence, God showed us what we would look like if we had to cover ourselves. Once everybody saw you for what you were, you realized that you could not cover yourself. So you came back saying, "Lord, just as I am."

Now you have humbled yourself.

IT IS YOUR CHOICE

As long as things are going well, you will never confess the sin in your life. You will never admit it, you will never own up to it. It is only when circumstances bring you down that you then will be humble under the hand of God.

You cannot walk around acting as if you are stronger than you really are.

You still have to keep coming to the altar every week.

Why?

Because the spirit of lying was greater than the spirit of truth. You kept lying to yourself until suddenly; the demons were exposed to show you that you had been protecting them.

All of this time, it was by choice.

WE'VE GOT THE BEAT

I remember an old church song we used to sing years ago when I was a kid. "All to Jesus, I surrender. All to Him, I freely give. I will ever love and trust Him, in His Presence daily life. I surrender all.

I surrender all. All to Thee, my Blessed Savior, I surrender all." The Church today does not want to hear songs like that. Those are *boring* songs. They have no beat.

My response to that is simple. Other songs may have beat but they cannot keep you out of sin, out of the flesh or off the corner. They cannot keep the drugs and alcohol out of your system.

They cannot keep you out of line up in the penal system. So many wonderful things appeal to the flesh, but they are not reaching our spirits. So we continue to perpetuate the same sins.

WHAT HAVE YOU DONE WITH WHAT YOU'VE ALREADY HEARD?

Some years ago, I preached a message entitled, "What Have You Done With What You've Already Heard?"

At that same time, so many people were saying, "Lord, give me more. I just want more God, more Word of God."

So God sent a Word to His House, saying, "What have you done with what you have already heard?"

You do not need more revelation until you have walked out what you have already gotten. God gives us instruction, and we are so ready to say, "And Lord, what's going to happen after that?"

He says, "Wait a minute. Do what I told you to do first."

However, we get frustrated with God and take matters into our own hands, simply because we will not take the first steps until He explains the second and third and fourth. What God is saying is that, if you can trust Him enough to do the first thing He tells you, the last part will be very obvious.

EVERY STAR, EVERY GRAIN OF SAND

In Genesis, God spoke to Abraham, saying:

Blessing I will bless you, and multiplying I will multiply your descendants as the stars of the heaven and as the sand which is on the seashore; and your descendants shall possess the gate of their enemies. [18]*In your seed all the nations of the earth shall be blessed, because you have obeyed My voice.*

(Genesis 22:17-18)

Upon hearing God's promises, Abraham said, "God, I only have one child in my house and that's my nephew. He's not even my own flesh and blood. How am I going to do this?"

God said, "Don't worry, I'm going to work this thing out in you. I am the God of all flesh and nothing is too hard for Me."

Then, in the course of time, three angels came and said, "Hey Abraham, guess what? Next year, at this time, your wife is going to have a child."

Keep in mind, Abraham was already an old man, about ninety-nine years old, and his wife was just ten years younger.

Sarah laughed at the thought.

The angels said "Why did you laugh?"

She said, "I'm old, and you know Abe, he sure isn't what he used to be."

The angels replied, "That's okay, by next year this time, you're going to have a child."

Sarah's flesh could not believe. Abraham could not believe. But the Almighty God performed the impossible despite the impossibilities confronting the candidates.

Sure enough, Sarah got pregnant! For someone holding this book now, your situation appears impossible. Seemingly, time is not on your side. But in the Name of the One Who holds time in His hands, I decree that the miraculous is about to work in your favor! As sure as the God who *"...changes the times and the seasons"*, lives, *The clock that worked against you will now begin to work for you in Jesus' Mighty Name*! (Daniel 2:21).

THE FIRST ONE IS ENOUGH

Why did I tell that long story?

Abraham did not live to see all his descendants as countless as the sand or the stars. But you know what he *did* see?

He saw his first child.

Here is the important thing: if you see the first one, you do not have to see the end of it. Why? Because it was already *impossible* for the first one to come. So if God does the impossible in the first thing, you do not have to worry about the rest of the way. All God is trying to get you and I to do, is to trust Him for that first step.

If He can make you take the first step, you do not have to worry about what the end of the thing is going to be. You never saw yourself taking the first step anyhow. God is trying to get you to stop looking to see the end of the story (Isaiah 46:10). All you need to do is say, "God just get something started." All you have to do is get the first seed, and it will go on from there.

WHAT PART DO YOU PLAY?

God has given me a vision of ministry hitting multiple areas, doing great thing that will impact the world. He has worked with me on this thing, though, because I had to realize something. What if He gave me the vision of it, and I am not going to be the one to live long enough to see it all?

But if I see the first church, that is enough.

Can you be content with the part that you play, even if you do not get recognition for being the "player"?

Can *you* be content with the "part"?

David got a chance to gather the material, but his son built the temple. That is why I fight so hard for my children, not necessarily because I think they are going to be the ones to fulfill that vision, but I know that if the enemy can cut them off in front of my face, he will show me that the vision for my family has already died. So I have to keep them in prayer with a godly standard before them as long as I am living. Even if I go off scene, at least I know I did my part, and I can die at peace, knowing that I have set things in motion.

THERE'S MORE TO IT THAN MEETS THE EYE

If you are feeling as if you do not know if this situation or circumstance is ever going to turn around, maybe you were not supposed to be the one to turn it around. Maybe you were supposed to live a holy standard so others would have something to fall back on. Be content that God at least enlisted you in the program.

Maybe you are not the one who is supposed to be the '*be all and end all*' for your child. But because you submitted to God's chastening, you are the one who showed him or her that it was okay to have confrontation with discipline to come. So now, he or she will be open for the Lords confrontation when their time comes.

There is always more to your purpose than you could ever have supposed.

I SURRENDER ALL OR DO YOU?

Maybe you desperately need a surrendered life. You may have to tell something or someone, "Though I love you, I might have to let go of you, because I cannot throw both my hands up and surrender while I am holding onto you. I cannot have my arms wrapped around your waist and still say, 'All to Jesus, I surrender.'"

Whatever I hold onto, when God is telling me to hold onto Him, I have made *that* thing my god and God is obligated to destroy it.

So how could I hold onto you and say that I love you when I know that what we have is against God?

What or who has God told you to let go of?

MOVING ON

If you have shaken off your demon and activated a plan to maintain that freedom, you are ready to move on.

It is my deepest prayer that you, dear reader, have now been set free from what was tormenting you.

Stand strong and soar in your new found victory!

PRAYER POINT

Father! Let me never again descend to the depths that You have so graciously lifted me from. In Jesus' Mighty Name, Amen!

SCRIPTURE REFERENCE:

Isaiah 40:31

PRAYER TO RECEIVE SALVATION

In order to start a productive relationship with God, you must surrender your life to the Lordship of Jesus Christ. If you have not accepted Jesus Christ as your Lord and Savior, I encourage you to pray the following prayer aloud in order to receive your salvation

Dear God, I come to you believing that Jesus died on the cross and was raised from the dead to save my soul. I ask you to come into my heart and change me from within enabling me to enter into Your way of living. I confess with my mouth that I believe Jesus died for me and I now receive Your gift of salvation. I am now born again. I confess that Jesus Christ is the Son of God and He is now the Lord of my life. Amen.

This is the wisest decision you have ever made. Please, do not look back. Endeavor to find a Bible-believing ministry where the unadulterated Word of God is being preached and taught. Begin to worship there regularly and attend Bible study. Be sure to read, study your bible and pray daily. Always ask the Holy Spirit to teach you His word before you study.

Welcome to the kingdom of light. May the Lord God bless and uphold you, in Jesus' Mighty Name! I am waiting to hear from you.

ABOUT THE AUTHOR

J.E Bamidele Sturdivant, Sr. is the pastor of Faith United Ministries and is known worldwide as a blessing to the body of Christ. His unique style of simply, yet powerfully conveying Biblical principles has drawn millions to the cross and set the stage for massive deliverances and healings in the lives of God's people.

A native Washingtonian, J.E Sturdivant has made a divine connection to Nigeria through his God-appointed relationship with his Father in the Lord, E.A Adeboye. Heralded by Newsweek as one of the 50 Most Powerful world leaders, Adeboye has fully received J.E Sturdivant as a special son and poured mightily into his life in immeasurable ways. Adeboye, with the care of a father, named J.E Sturdivant "Bamidele," which is translated to mean *follow me home.*

Their relationship mirrors that of prophet Elijah and his protégé, Elisha. As with these Biblical men of God, Bamidele has seen the ascension of Adeboye to greater heights in the Lord. In turn, the same mantle has fallen on him. Since their divine connection, Bamidele's ministry has been marked by the miraculous. Countless testimonies of actual resurrections from the dead, healing from cancer and astounding breakthroughs on every level speak to the authenticity of God's hand on his life and ministry.

A master teacher, Bamidele diligently studies to show himself worthy unto God and in the process earned degrees in Ministry. In turn, the sound Biblical truths he shares undoubtedly remind the world that holiness and excellence are the true hallmark of every Christ-follower.

An accomplished author, Bamidele has written *No Longer Crippled…From Trauma To Triumph*!, which outlines the blueprint for a wholistically, successful life. He also authored sections of *From One Brother To Another*, an inspirational devotional for men of all ethnicities, ages, and social backgrounds. His most recent release, *"A Divine Hunger"*, challenges every believer to live a life of holiness supported by an appetite for the Master's Presence.

He was selected as the Guest Chaplain to offer prayer in the United States Senate in the presence of President Barack Obama, who was serving as United States Senator from Illinois at the time. His anointed and dynamic preaching style has also garnered the attention of other political officials.

He is a greatly esteemed and sought after evangelist who frequently ministers extensively throughout North America, the Caribbean, Africa, Asia, and Europe. J.E Bamidele and his wife, Pamela D, have been married for over 32 years and are the proud parents of four adult children.

You can contact J.E Bamidele Sturdivant using the mediums listed below. Although he cannot respond personally to all correspondences, he would love to get your feedback.

J.E.S. Ministries

7905 Fernham Lane,

District Heights

Maryland 20747

USA

Phone: 301-736-2383

Email: pastor@jesturdivantministries.org

Website: www.jesturdivantministries.org

Please include your testimony of help received from this book when you write. Your prayer requests are welcome.

OTHER BOOKS BY THE MINISTRY

No Longer Crippled

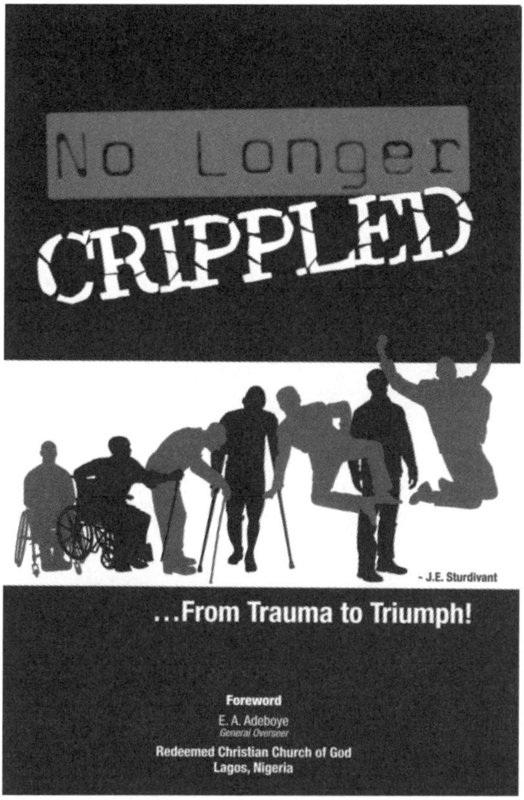

Adversity. It's one of the guarantees that come with being human. We experience it. We expect it. But it's how we choose to deal with it that shapes our lives, both negatively and positively. Adversity can leave us crippled in our emotions, our relationships, and our finances. However, God, in all His grace, equips us with the prescription and therapy to heal us in those hurting areas. In this book, J.E. Sturdivant shows us that with God working and moving in our lives, we can triumph and use adversity to our advantage.

A Divine Hunger

A Divine Hunger is a piece that will challenge you to grow in your walk with God. It is full of revelation knowledge from God's word on how to develop a hunger and a heart for the word, keep your mind on the word, live by the word and be liberated by the word. Many run helter skelter looking for solutions to their personal problems but the most enduring way to be secured in life is to develop an intimate relationship with God through His word.

Our lives glorify God when we bear fruit as we abide in Him and His words remain in us. This is only possible when we unreservedly commit to Him and value the relationship with Him above anything else in the world. No matter how gloomy your circumstances may be, this book will energize you and help you to experience the abundant life in all your endeavors. Be blessed as you read.

Impacting Your World

The whole world is going into chaos because God's children are not manifesting their God-given ability. To operate on the level which God has destined for us, He requires that we know Him more intimately and walk in His ways. The primary way to know God is through His Word. *Impacting Your World* is a tool that will help you to grow in your relationship with God by meditating on His Word.

God's grace is imparted on us in an increasing measure as we go deeper into His Word. Confessing the Word only becomes a major part of *faith release* if the process of *faith formation* has been completed in the course of meditation. In this book, J.E Bamidele Sturdivant clearly outlines that speaking the truth of God's Word, works together with our faith to bring victory every time!

WATCH OUT! THE FOLLOWING BOOKS ARE TO BE RELEASED SHORTLY BY THE MINISTRY

1. Hearing and Knowing God's Voice

2. What does your flesh have to say?

3. Recognizing When the Devil Speaks
(*Silencing the voice of the enemy*)

4. More than a CONQUEROR (*Winning Spiritual Warfare*)

5. Peace